FINANCING FOR DEVELOPMENT:
PROPOSALS FROM BUSINESS AND CIVIL SOCIETY

Financing for Development:

Proposals from Business and Civil Society

Edited by:

BARRY HERMAN

FEDERICA PIETRACCI and

KRISHNAN SHARMA

United Nations

**United Nations
University Press**

TOKYO • NEW YORK • PARIS

© The United Na............ University Press, 2001

The views expressed in this publication are those of the authors and do not necessarily reflect the views of the United Nations University or the United Nations.

United Nations University Press
The United Nations University, 53-70, Jingumae 5-chome
Shibuya-ku, Tokyo, 150-8925, Japan
Tel: +81-3-3499-2811   Fax: +81-3-3406-7345
E-mail: sales@hq.unu.edu
http://www.unu.edu

United Nations University Office in North America
2 United Nations Plaza, Room DC2-1462-70, New York, NY 10017, USA
Tel: +1-212-963-6387   Fax: +1-212-371-9454
E-mail: unuona@igc.apc.org

United Nations University Press is the publishing division of the United Nations University.

Cover design by Joyce C. Weston

Printed in Hong Kong

UNUP-1073
ISBN 92-808-1073-1

Library of Congress Cataloging-in-Publication Data

Financing for development: proposals from business and civil society / edited by Barry Herman, Federica Pietracci, Krishnan Sharma.

p.   cm.

Includes bibliographical references and index.

ISBN 9280810731 (pbk.)

1. Investments, Foreign—Developing countries. 2. Economic development—Finance. 3. Finance—Developing countries. 4. International finance.
I. Herman, Barry. II. Pietracci, Federica. III. Sharma, Krishnan.

HG5993 .F559 2001

338.91—dc21

2001005191

CONTENTS

CONTENTS

PREFACE

We live in an era of rapid change. One central component of that change is the process of globalization. Globalization has created enormous wealth for some in many parts of the world, but it has also left many behind. NGOs have been at the forefront of pointing to the downsides of globalization, whether it was through articles, the Internet or, more recently, the streets of Seattle and Genoa. Regrettably, this has at times been accompanied by violence.

There are legitimate concerns about the workings of the world economy, the depth of poverty, inequalities and marginalization. The United Nations is in a unique position to engage in a constructive dialogue, not only with those who are most critical of the workings of the international economy, but also with those who drive the international economy, i.e., the business sector.

The United Nations is currently preparing for an unprecedented conference that addresses the interlocking issues of financing and development in the context of globalization. This International Conference on Financing for Development, to be held in Monterrey, Mexico in March 2002, offers an extremely important opportunity to create a new international partnership for a more equitable economic and financial governance of the world economy. This partnership cannot be reached without the participation of "all relevant stakeholders". This, of course, includes the Governments of the Member States of the United Nations and all appropriate official international organizations, but it also includes the business sector and civil society.

The present book is a case in point. Compiled after hearings held in the General Assembly as part of the preparatory process for the International Conference, it includes a broad sample of views and aims to facilitate a discussion among all interested parties about the future directions of globalization and development. As readers will see, the question of financing seems to impinge on all aspects of both subjects. Different readers will approve or reject different proposals that are made here. That is as it should be. That is the nature of debate. I myself do not necessarily agree with all of the ideas expressed here. But it is crucial that readers appreciate the concerns that motivate the proposals, assess the analyses critically and sharpen their own thinking about global policy needs. That is precisely the kind of active engagement the forthcoming conference needs if it is to succeed.

Kofi A. Annan
Secretary-General
of the United Nations

ACKNOWLEDGEMENTS

This book is appearing because quite a few people believe something important is happening at the United Nations regarding the initiative called "financing for development" and they wanted to help support it. Above all are the authors of the essays in this book, who volunteered the time and effort, firstly, to participate in the hearings organized for the United Nations Preparatory Committee for the International Conference on Financing for Development. They all patiently and quickly worked with us to revise their presentations for this volume. As editors, we can say we thoroughly enjoyed working with each of them. We also wish to express our appreciation to the other participants in the hearings whose statements we could not include owing to space limitations.

It is one thing to produce a manuscript for publication and it is quite another to produce the book itself and do it so expeditiously. For this, we are indebted to the United Nations University Press, its head, Ms. Janet Boileau, and her capable staff. The manuscript was ably copy-edited, probably in record time, by Ms. Elizabeth Lara of the United Nations and the index was prepared by Ms. Angela Cottingham. We are also very grateful to Mr. Valerian Monteiro for design and typesetting of the book, to Ms. Remedios Catolico, Mr. Kalu Odege and Ms. Maria Consuelo (Suzette) Limchoc for their quiet efficiency in preparing the manuscripts, as well as to the many staff and interns of the Department of Economic and Social Affairs who were pressed into service for proofreading. Colleagues like these made it a pleasure to work on this book.

Introduction

*BARRY HERMAN, FEDERICA PIETRACCI
AND KRISHNAN SHARMA[1]*

In the present volume, representatives of business and civil society offer advice to policy makers on how to improve financing for development. Most financing in most developing countries involves private enterprises, whether in the formal or informal sectors, whether domestic or foreign. Even so, the public sector plays a major role in directly financing some activities and in policy guidance over others. The nature of the public role and the content of public policies are of prime concern to all parties interested in financing for development. This book brings together a diverse set of assessments and proposals from the business sector and civil society in different parts of the world by individuals who are concerned about what public institutions and policies should be attempting to do to facilitate and accelerate the financing of development.

1. The policy context of "financing for development"

The starting point in thinking about the public role in financing for development is that private markets exist within institutional frameworks that are created and maintained by governments and the international organizations they establish. It is also relevant that those markets are generally guided by policies that the official bodies determine. Beyond this is the direct public provision of financial resources, and, indeed, governments and their international organizations undertake numerous types of financing that are important sources of funding in many developing countries. Thus, both directly and indirectly, governments and international institutions help to shape the

---

[1]   Department of Economic and Social Affairs of the United Nations Secretariat. Views expressed herein are those of the authors and not necessarily those of the United Nations.

financing of development, even in a world of largely private economic activity.

The globalization of the world economy—the liberalized and rapidly expanding movement among countries of goods, services and finance—has been an especially important factor in recent years in shaping the opportunities for the financing of development. Globalization has produced great economic opportunities that some economies have successfully taken advantage of; but it has also posed great challenges, especially for development and its financing.

The now-familiar demonstrators in the streets trying to shut down official international meetings dealing with the financial and trading system and development are only the most visible of people with serious concerns and critiques. The activities of governments in promoting globalization and in integrating into the world economy have been lauded by some and heavily criticized by others. The demonstrators largely argue that governments and their international institutions do not intervene enough to ameliorate the social and environmental—indeed, the developmental—costs of globalization. Other critics say that the best way to help people and promote development in the new world economy is to accelerate the retreat of direct policy interventions from economic activity. Globalization and the controversies it has created have made it easy to argue that governments should do more to make national economies and the international financial and trading systems work more effectively to improve the human condition. But exactly what should they do? That is not so clear.

There is not a full consensus, in other words, about many of the dimensions of economic policy that pertain to financing for development. The financial crises and disappointments of the past several years have reduced confidence in many of the official recommendations that were offered with great conviction only five years ago, especially in the realm of financial policy. Equally, when the cold war ended, the depth of "aid fatigue" was unmasked, and levels of official development assistance dropped sharply. We do not believe the impulse for aid arising from the sense of shared humanity was in any way lessened. It was rather a loss of confidence in the aid relationship and in the conditions donors required in exchange for financial support. These challenges to the conventional wisdom on financing for development have created a new fluidity in the "marketplace of ideas" and an important opening for international consideration of proposals that have not yet been accorded consensus status or embodied in policy.

This publication seeks to contribute to such consideration by presenting the views of authors representing 21 institutions or organizations that espouse very different ideas about financing for development. They come from different ends of the political spectrum and from several different countries of the

North and South. Some of the chapters speak from a business or financial industry perspective, and others speak as "civil society". Some of the latter are from church-based organizations, others from secular development agencies and still others from academia, albeit working closely with civil society organizations. None of the authors speak for governments.

All of the authors speak for sustainable human development as they see it. All value highly the goal of poverty eradication that has become a centrepiece of international cooperation for development. All of them are sincere and honourable and their analyses deserve to be considered seriously. However, not all of them can be correct, especially as they sometimes disagree strongly. Nonetheless, on some issues they are much closer than might have been thought and closer than perhaps has been realized by advocates from the business and civil-society communities themselves.

2. Background to the book

The chapters in this book began as statements that the authors made to a committee of the General Assembly of the United Nations in November and December 2000 during hearings it held to solicit views from business and civil society on how to strengthen the financing of development.[2] The committee that organized the hearings had been charged by the General Assembly to prepare a unique intergovernmental conference on financing for development (FfD), which will take place in Monterrey, Mexico, in March 2002. The conference will be neither an academic discussion nor an occasion for broad declarations of norms. Governments do not meet for academic dispute, and the norms that guide FfD were already agreed upon by the 147 heads of State and Government who participated in the Millennium Assembly, held at the United Nations in September 2000, where the Millennium Declaration was adopted, as well as by the Governments that participated in earlier conferences in the 1990s.[3]

---

[2]   The 21 papers in this collection were selected by the editors from the 39 statements given at the hearings. They were chosen in order to include a representative range of views from a broad variety of stakeholders, while minimizing repetition and keeping within the strict space limitations of the present volume. Authors selected were given the opportunity to revise and update their papers and the chapters thus represent their views as of the time this book went to press. For summaries of the full hearings, including floor discussions, see "Financing for development: hearings with civil society, 6 and 7 November 2000" (A/AC.257/18) and "Financing for development: hearings with the business community, 11 and 12 December 2000" (A/AC.257/19).

[3]   See "United Nations Millennium Declaration", General Assembly resolution 55/2, adopted 8 September 2000, and *The World Conferences: Developing Priorities for the 21ˢᵗ Century,* Briefing Paper (New York, United Nations, 1997).

Instead, the Monterrey meeting will seek to reach agreement on a number of concrete steps to foster financing for development in its many dimensions.

With this aim in view, the FfD preparatory committee has sought and continues to seek to draw on the experiences and analyses of non-governmental practitioners and policy advocates from around the globe. While, ultimately, it is the governments that will have to agree to whatever steps they decide to take in Monterrey, the philosophy of the preparations has all along been to seriously involve "all relevant stakeholders". Besides the States Members of the United Nations and all the major international organizations dealing with financing and development, this has included the views of business and finance, and of non-governmental organizations that have been active in development work.[4]

The role of non-state actors in FfD is part of a rather striking departure from traditional practice that has been taking place at the United Nations in recent years, and that is being reflected to greater or lesser degree in other international organizations. Through most of its history, United Nations meetings have been almost exclusively meetings of government representatives. There have always been exceptions in special areas such as human rights or in special forums such as the Economic and Social Council, but these practices were limited. Generally, it could be assumed that non-State actors could influence their governments in national political processes and that the governments could then bring the results to the international body. Hence, exceptions aside, there was no need for a special role for civil society. Today, however, many official meetings of the United Nations, such as FfD, have actively solicited the independent views of non-State actors.

One reason for this is that civil-society activists and business leaders have actively sought to influence the United Nations and other international institutions independently of influencing national governments in their capitals. In part this reflects a perception, which is probably exaggerated, that international organizations have a measure of independence of their government overseers. In part, however, it also reflects a perception that governments in capitals can be influenced through their representatives at the United Nations, as well as vice versa. In so doing, one marshals arguments at the United Nations that use a different language from that used in national capitals. One can unabashedly couch one's argument at the United Nations in terms of humanity's needs, one's obligations to the planet, the moral imperative of fighting

[4]   For additional details, see Barry Herman, "Civil society and the financing for development initiative at the United Nations," in *Civil Society and Global Finance*, Jan Aart Scholte with Albrecht Schnabel, eds., (Tokyo, United Nations University Press, forthcoming).

global poverty. This is a harder case to make in the capitals, where the main focus is quite naturally the national interest.

In addition, however, many governments have come to see advantages to their own national positions and interests from the active involvement of non-State actors in the United Nations and other bodies. There is a sense that civil society activists may be closer to the "grassroots" than some governments and that they may support political forces within governments to push for policies that reflect the universal values espoused at the United Nations. Civil-society organizations can thus bring relevant expertise and a political presence to the international negotiating table, even if they cannot vote in the deliberations themselves.

By the same token, businesses—whether domestic or multinational—generally seek independence from government in carrying out the activities of private enterprise. Governments now universally seek to promote such enterprise, and thus government representatives also see business-sector spokespersons as having relevant expertise to bring to the table. They also bring economic, if not political, power in that individual businesses decide whether and where to operate, always expecting and usually receiving compensation for so doing in the form of profit.

The chapters that follow this introduction are grouped thematically, and each group includes views from business and civil-society authors, as appropriate. There are, however, certain perceptions and concerns that can be associated more with the business community or with civil society, and these shared views might fruitfully be highlighted as well.

3. The perspective of business executives

In the chapters in this collection authored by business executives, one will find certain common themes. The most basic is on the role of government in the broadest sense in establishing and maintaining an "enabling environment" for private economic activity. An appropriate environment will provide the strongest foundation for a favourable climate for local and foreign investment, in this view.

First and foremost among the aspects of an enabling environment, according to business-sector authors, is the need for countries to have a robust and favourable legal and regulatory infrastructure facing local and foreign companies alike. It should provide adequate transparency with respect to rules, transactions, macro and micro conditions, projects and potential partners. Cheryl Hesse (Capital International), Marshall Carter (State Street Bank), Andre van Heemstra (Unilever) and Tom Marshella (Moody's Investors Service) outline the different requirements of foreign investors in this area. Chulakorn Singhakowin (Bank of Asia) and Victor Valdepeñas (UnionBank of the Philippines) provide a developing-country perspective on the importance of having appropriate legal, regulatory and transparency conditions.

From the viewpoint of participants in foreign financial markets, Hesse and Carter point out the increased attention being paid by investors, in the aftermath of the Asian crisis, to corporate governance in emerging markets. Overall, Carter recommends policies that reduce the "relationship-oriented" component in finance that is evident in many developing countries and instead make it more "arms-length". According to Hesse, the characteristics of good corporate governance comprise transparency, equitable treatment of shareholders and accountability. Carter further elaborates on this by stressing the need for increased financial disclosure under internationally recognized accounting standards, a globally acceptable legal framework, coherent bankruptcy codes and financial market supervision.

The institutional reforms linked to strengthening transparency, legal systems and regulation are also important to foreign direct investors, such as van Heemstra. Before making a long-term commitment of resources, investors want to know the "rules of the game". In addition, they want to know that the rules will be enforced fairly and efficiently, and that they will not be changed capriciously. In particular, Marshella points to the importance to creditors helping to finance large projects of having a stable legal and regulatory regime that is capable of consistently enforcing legal obligations and providing remedies to bond holders in the event of their violation. He outlines the conditions for a return of investor interest in financing infrastructure projects in Asia. These conditions include a freer and more frequent flow of information on the financial and operating performance of individual projects.

From the perspective of a Thai banker, Chulakorn argues that the entire financial and banking reform that is being undertaken in Thailand depends upon the successful reforms in the overall institutional environment. He stresses the importance of having an appropriate legal and regulatory infrastructure to support Thailand's market-led financial reform process, pointing out that the clearance of bad loans from the banking system has been slow owing to a still weak legal set-up. Despite Government efforts to reform insolvency and bankruptcy codes, laws and court procedures remained insufficient to resolve problem loans on a timely basis or to deter new defaults. Chulakorn also points out that that there is a need for further consolidation of the Thai financial sector, which would be facilitated by revision of regulations that deter market-driven mergers and acquisitions.

Victor Valdepeñas looks at the issue of financial reform from the viewpoint of a Philippine banker. He calls for the development of domestic capital markets in the Philippines, especially debt markets, in order to promote risk diversification and reduce over-dependence of local companies upon banks. The ability to do this, however, is contingent upon reforms linked to transparency, legal systems and regulation. For instance, shortcomings in transparency and inadequate protection of creditors and shareholders are likely to dissuade local and foreign investors from placing funds in local currency bond and equity markets.[5]

Valdepeñas explicitly includes within the definition of "transparency" more information and data on corporate transactions. This would be of benefit to banks through limiting risk (without eliminating it, which is neither possible nor desirable) and reducing chances of panic in emerging financial markets from lack of information. Valdepeñas argues that the Asian financial crisis was rooted in an excessive build-up of market risks, in particular, greater foreign exchange exposures in the corporate balance sheet that became possible with capital account liberalization. To better understand these new forms of risk arising in the private sector, he points out that it is necessary to have new analytics, new measures and information tools, new monitoring systems to track these new measures and new risk-management infrastructure. Valdepeñas therefore proposes a new national monitoring system that tracks corporate balance sheets and embedded risks, as well as other indicators of importance, such as the investments and risk exposures of non-resident investors in the country.

Also important to business speakers is the extent and quality of the physical and human infrastructure. Thus, Rodney Harper (Alcatel) focuses on how the revolution in communications and information technology can be spread to the developing world, thereby bridging the "digital divide" between industrialized and developing countries. He recommends that unified action should be developed under the auspices of the United Nations—between governments, the private sector, financial institutions, service/content providers, suppliers and non-governmental organizations (NGOs)—with the objective being to identify, define, finance, engineer, build and support sustainable communications projects in the developing world. However, complementary support for this would be needed at a country level, through the development of a coherent

---

[5] Shortcomings in transparency and the strong relationships between banks, companies and governments in many South-East Asian countries also dissuade issuance of corporate bonds (see Krishnan Sharma, "The underlying constraints on corporate bond market development in South-East Asia", *World Development,* vol. 29, No. 8, August 2001).

information and communications technology strategy by the governments concerned. Governments should also initiate efforts to develop an affordable telecommunications infrastructure and an appropriately educated workforce.

In sum, the discussion on an enabling domestic environment for the private sector points to some common requirements by both foreign investors and local businesses. Taking this point a step further, it can be argued that a thriving domestic enterprise sector can be an important positive signal to consumer and manufacturing-based direct investors and portfolio investors.

Another set of issues covered in some of the papers concerns the willingness of corporations to work in a framework consistent with sustainable development. In this respect, Andre van Heemstra makes an interesting point that policies designed by the governments of developing countries attract foreign direct investment by easing regulatory standards on environment, safety and treatment of workers would be counter-productive. Rather, companies such as Unilever would be unwilling to invest in markets in which weak regulation and enforcement allow others to gain a competitive advantage by operating to standards that they find unacceptable.

However, the sine qua non for business is profit, and businesses are only able to operate so as to advance broader development objectives, in the view of their spokesmen, if this is consistent with profit-making goals. On this note, Hanns Michael Hoelz (Deutsche Bank) insists that the two objectives are mutually compatible in emerging markets. Hoelz stresses that it is in the interests of multinationals that their plans include a measure of long-term investment in the social development of developing countries, since the momentum of growth arising from globalization cannot be sustained unless it results in benefits for the world's people. At the same time, before investing, multinationals should have a broader commitment to sustainable development and the incorporation of environmental factors in their risk assessment.

Hoelz's suggestion is that social investment is best achieved through strong operating partnerships with organizations at the local level, with civil society, governments, international organizations and donors. Moreover, the coordination and implementation of many policies should take place at the grassroots level. Social investment, in particular, could entail the strategic deployment of capital through microfinance schemes as a tool to enable disadvantaged communities to enter the economic mainstream.

John de Wit, who heads a microfinance organization in South Africa that provides credit for the poor (Small Enterprise Foundation), views microcredit and enterprise development from up close. De Wit argues that the authorities in developing countries should not pressure commercial banks to enter the field of microcredit, which is a highly specialized field. Rather, governments should make the activity viable for microcredit operators by relaxing general restrictions on lending activities and, within limits, on interest rate ceilings on loans. The strategy for promoting microcredit should be long-term and based on building sound foundations for the sector. While sufficient funding should be provided by the authorities, they nevertheless need to ensure that there is no unwarranted political interference in the operations of the microcredit sector and that support does not become the captive of unrelated political calculations. Moreover, according to de Wit, microcredit schemes will be more successful if they are complemented by measures to enhance the ability of the poor to borrow and undertake business ventures. Their ability is lessened if they are constantly vulnerable to economic shocks and natural disasters and if they cannot deal effectively with the normal burden of life-cycle expenditures. He thus called on developing country governments to promote greater savings and insurance services for the poor.

Finally, some suggestions are made with respect to international trade. Van Heemstra in his paper emphasizes the benefits that regional integration can have in attracting foreign direct investment. In addition, Tom Niles (United States Council for International Business) stresses the need for developed countries to show leadership in dismantling agricultural protection citing, in particular, the United States and the Common Agricultural Policy in Europe. For Niles, the African Growth and Opportunity Act adopted by the United States represents, in spite of its limitations, an important first step in increasing access to the United States market. At the same time, all countries should adopt the principles of corporate governance of the Organisation for Economic Cooperation and Development and eliminate the corruption and bribery rampant in many countries.

In sum, a number of interesting suggestions are contained in the chapters originating in the business sector. Some of these issues have come to the fore in national and international policy discussions during the past few years, especially the legal and regulatory framework relating to corporate governance, transparency, the concept of corporate citizenship and trade-related issues. Although other themes, such as those relating to stability, infrastructure and microcredit, have been with us for some time, these chapters highlight new and varied perspectives on them. There are, of course, still many more issues that have not been incorporated here. Nevertheless, we believe that the sample of views and proposals represent an important beginning in understanding and taking account of what may be called the perspective of business in the policy dialogue on financing for development.

4. The perspective of civil society advocates

Civil society embodies a heterogeneous collection of non-governmental viewpoints, yet the civil society speakers at the General Assembly hearings—and those selected for inclusion in this book, in particular—shared a number of policy priorities. Within an overall focus on poverty eradication, several speakers emphasized the linkage of domestic to international policy, which led to proposals aimed at curbing the volatility in the financial system, democratizing the decision-making processes of the international financial institutions, dealing comprehensively with the debt crises of developing countries, and increasing the role of the United Nations in economic policy matters. At the same time, proposals were addressed to governments of developing countries. In some cases, a particular concern was seen to require thinking and action at both domestic and international levels. In particular, a number of presenters highlighted the need for a gender analysis of economic and financial issues. They argued that the gender aspects of trade, access to capital, structural adjustment conditionalities and decision-making needed to be addressed systematically.

In this context, Zo Randriamaro (Third World Network-Africa) and Douglas Hellinger, Karen Hansen-Kuhn and April Fehling (Development Group for Alternative Policies) emphasize the need to take "pro-poor" initiatives. Randriamaro discusses the need to mobilize and retain domestic financial resources to support local production, as opposed to financial liberalization, especially for small and medium-scale enterprises in strategic sectors of the economy such as agriculture, with a particular focus on its effects on women. Randriamaro points out the limitations of microfinance and its impact on women, and discusses the real danger of further marginalization of the poor and women under the current poverty reduction strategies. She therefore recommends that the State should provide an innovative and supportive institutional framework for economic growth and sustainable and equitable human development. Hellinger, and others, challenge the nature of decision-making and the way in which the imposition of structural adjustment programmes has undermined democratic processes, increased poverty and inequality, and generated social, economic and financial instability. They do this in the context of assessing the poverty effects of economic policies, showcasing four country examples (Bolivia, Burkina Faso, Mozambique and Tanzania).

Mariama Williams (Development Alternatives with Women for a New Era, DAWN) and Roberto Rubio-Fabián (National Development

Foundation of El Salvador) focus on institutional and policy reform in developing countries. Williams argues that trade liberalization and foreign investment do not "work". This is because the assumed positive links between trade, direct investment, poverty and gender do not necessarily exist. There is need for an explicit, integrated framework for sustainable, gender-sensitive human development, in her view. This integrated framework should link trade, debt and investment (including capital flows). Williams stresses also that efforts to mobilize international financial resources in the form of private capital flows and trade should be undertaken in a context that does not exacerbate the current trend towards privatizing social and public goods. Rubio stresses that, in mobilizing domestic resources, the key question on which to focus is how such resources should be used. What priorities countries plan to finance and how they finance those priorities are as important as where they obtain the requisite funding. Explaining how El Salvador developed its national plan, he underscores the role of institutional innovation and social inclusion in transforming budgetary processes into quality national investments consistent with human development goals, the preservation of ecosystems and the basic needs of the poor and the excluded.

Tariq Banuri and Erika Spanger-Siegfried (Regional and International Networking Group [The Ring]) address the theme of creating and building the capacity to use financial resources effectively. They make a distinction between what they call the traditional "supply-side" approach to finance, preoccupied with the mobilization of concessional resources, and an alternative "demand-side" approach that focuses instead on creating the ability, especially of small and medium-scale entities, to access and deploy financial resources on commercial terms. They argue that the experience at local level in programmes and projects of sustainable livelihoods, poverty eradication and natural resource conservation shows that the donor support for such economic capacity-building would often be far more effective and relevant than the direct provision of concessional assistance. They thus propose a three-pronged approach that includes reversing the trajectory of declining sources of finance, creating an institutional framework that will enable and encourage private, non-concessional finance to reach small and medium-scale enterprises, and strengthening the ability of small and medium-scale borrowers to access and deploy resources effectively.

Macroeconomic policy-making was also discussed by civil society speakers. Marina Ponti and Davide Zanoni (Mani Tese) ask whether a liberalized financial market is beneficial to all, and challenge how the "policy trilemma" is resolved. That is, economists can demonstrate that it is impossible to achieve simultaneously free capital mobility, a pegged exchange rate and an independent monetary policy. Ponti and Zanoni advocate giving up free capital movements. Instead, they propose "capital controls" in the form of financial disincentives (based on the Chilean model) to reduce vulnerability of national financial systems. In this respect, they argue that measures should be specifically designed in accordance with the conditions in individual countries.

In this regard, Bart Bode (Broederlijk Delen) calls for the introduction of a currency transaction tax (CTT) that would apply a modest rate in normal times and a punitive rate to discourage international flows during a financial crisis. CTT can be a tool for prudential regulation, for protection against speculative attacks on national currency and for releasing some of the immobile central bank reserves for investment in domestic social development. According to Bode, the introduction of CTT could also have an ethical aspect as it would be a tax on capital as opposed to the disproportionate taxing of labour. Applied globally, Bode claims the CTT could raise significant resources for social development in developed and developing countries.

Other speakers of both the North and South also considered taxation issues. Recommendations included transforming domestic fiscal machineries to capture lost revenue for development, minimizing tax avoidance on the part of multinational corporations and implementing a currency transaction tax to curb financial volatility and raise revenue for social development.

Jenny Kimmis and Ruth Mayne (Oxfam GB) introduce the issue of international tax competition and tax havens, both of which are inadequately addressed under the current system of global economic governance. Kimmis and Mayne propose four policy options that could help the international community deal with these problems: (a) signing a multilateral agreement to share information on tax matters; (b) supporting the proposal for an international convention to facilitate the recovery and repatriation of funds illegally appropriated from national treasuries of poor countries; (c) agreeing to allow States to tax multinationals on a global unitary basis, with appropriate mechanisms to allocate tax revenues internationally and help avoid transfer pricing abuses; and (d) setting up a global tax authority to gather information, serve as a forum for discussing international tax policy issues, use peer pressure to bring tax-free riders into line, and develop codes of conduct based on best practices in tax issues.

Jens Martens (World Economy, Ecology and Development) stresses the urgency of reversing the reduction in the level of official development assistance by creating a new political framework, grounded in the concept of solidarity.

Martens suggests implementing this concept through intercountry income transfers (e.g., a progressive income tax on rich countries), which would increase the reliability as well as the amount of official resources and ease long-term development planning in the South. He further proposes that to avoid a return to excessive indebtedness of heavily indebted countries that receive debt relief, development assistance should be in non-repayable grant form.

On the issue of debt, contributors offered a variety of views, including outright repudiation of debt and the formation of debtors' coalitions to maximize the benefits from the debt initiative for highly indebted poor countries. Kunibert Raffer (University of Vienna) puts forward a major proposal on debt arbitration, which has been embraced by the Jubilee 2000 campaign. Raffer discusses how a fair and open process of arbitration can solve the debt problem, and proposes to constitute a neutral arbitration panel for each crisis country, with the creditors and the debtor each nominating an equal number of arbitrators, who in turn elect one more member who would break any tie vote. After the panel accomplished its task, it would be dissolved. Raffer argues that the United Nations can serve as the organization where such sovereign debtors can file their requests for arbitration, fairly balancing the interests of creditors and debtors, organizing the nomination of arbitrators and possibly providing limited secretariat services for arbitrators.

Perhaps the broadest proposed international initiative is to reform the United Nations itself. Julian Disney (International Council on Social Welfare) proposes various reforms of the Economic and Social Council, including improving basic access to the Council and its Bureau, developing expert high-level working groups, restructuring the Council itself or replacing it with a new Council, and lastly strengthening interaction with regional groupings.

In sum, the policy proposals contained in the 11 selected civil society papers underscore the degree to which FfD issues have come onto the agenda of organizations of concerned citizens and independent individuals engaged in development research, advocacy and practice. They have proposed policy initiatives that, in their view, take into account what works and what does not work based on experiences in development. Although typically starting at the social development end of the policy spectrum, their frustrations with the financing of development have drawn these activists to consider financial policy reforms. Their commitment to development leads them to ask big questions and they do not hesitate to propose big changes. In some cases, they may well be warranted.

5. Conclusion

One objective in seeking publication of this collection of views is to foster their discussion among a broad range of potentially interested parties. It is the hope of the editors that civil society advocates will pick up this book, not only to read what their colleagues have written, but also to read what the business people have to say. It is equally our hope that readers in the business community take to heart the concerns of the civil society advocates that are contained in this volume.

We are not expecting the various advocates whose views are represented in this book to forge common positions on most issues. Neither do we expect them to agree to work in harmonious partnership, except perhaps on a limited number of specific concerns. The interests, priorities and even understandings of how the world works are too different for that. From our perspective, that is not a problem but a source of strength. It is the responsibility of the policy makers to reach appropriate decisions on policy design and implementation, and they are best served by frank presentations of views that reflect complex reality. The art of policy making, after all, is to somehow arrive at the best judgements when opinions differ about what to do and how to do it.

Part One:

INITIATIVES FOCUSING ON THE POOR

1

Supportive domestic policies for microcredit

JOHN DE WIT[1]

This chapter deals with domestic policy issues that affect the provision of microcredit. It must be emphasized that the term microcredit strictly applies to the supply of micro-loans for income generation or enterprise development and very specifically not micro-loans for consumption.

The experiences of the Small Enterprise Foundation, a South African NGO, in terms of its interaction with the policy environment are presented here. From these experiences, recommendations are extrapolated that are believed to be pertinent not only for South Africa but for much of the developing world.

1. The Small Enterprise Foundation

The mission of the Small Enterprise Foundation (SEF) is the elimination of poverty. The organization, which began operations in 1992, is active in South Africa's rural areas where some 64 per cent of the population live below the poverty line and some 40 per cent below half the poverty line. [2]

The principle methodology used is group-based microcredit. In group-based lending, personal guarantees by a small, five-person group replace the conventional lending requirement for collateral. The organization has learned much from the Grameen Bank of Bangladesh, the pioneer organization in poverty alleviation through microcredit, and much of SEF's work is

---

[1] Managing Director, Small Enterprise Foundation, South Africa.

[2] The "household subsistence" level in South Africa is used as the poverty line. Currently this stands at 920 rand (US$130) per family of five per month.

patterned after that of the Grameen Bank. Since inception, SEF has disbursed in excess of 57,000 loans while maintaining an excellent recovery performance of less than 0.1 per cent bad debts over this period. Currently SEF serves 12,500 poor clients.

SEF is also somewhat unique in that it has been particularly dedicated not only to building an efficient microcredit programme but it has also focused on the very difficult task of specifically identifying the very poor, defined as those who live below half the poverty line, and ensuring that its programme has a positive impact on this group. The organization's poverty-targeting approach is regarded as a pioneer effort in the world of microcredit. The organization is frequently consulted on this work and has been asked to train others in this approach. As a result of SEF's leading role in championing microcredit for the very poor, the author has been asked to serve on the Policy Advisory Group of the Consultative Group to Assist the Poorest.[3]

2. The policy environment in South Africa

Possibly unlike some other contexts, the policy environment in South Africa has thus far not been a major obstacle for the development of microcredit. However, the Government's attempts to be pro-active and to facilitate improved access to microcredit, have largely failed. In that sense it is interesting to look at South Africa, as it contributes by pointing to some policy solutions but also shows the greater difficulties involved when government attempts to facilitate solutions.

The first microcredit organizations began in South Africa in the late 1980s. These were all non-governmental organizations, and this was the time of the apartheid regime. The NGOs simply ignored the majority of legislation that would have been a hindrance to their work. It was only with the establishment of legitimate government in South Africa that the organizations had to grapple with the policy environment.

3. Key aspects of the policy environment

The following aspects of the policy environment will be considered: restrictions on engaging in lending activities; interest rate limitations (the Usury Act); and pro-active steps (creating a supportive environment; government funding of microcredit; government and postal banks).

---

[3]   The Consultative Group to Assist the Poorest (CGAP) is a joint multilateral and bilateral forum housed at the World Bank. It was created to bring coherence to the activities of international donors in microfinance and to serve as a centre of excellence for the growth of a viable microfinance industry, with a specific focus on reaching the very poor.

Restrictions on engaging in lending activities

In some countries the law restricts who may or may not engage in lending activities, or it places certain restrictions on such activities. Whereas legislation around interest rates is needed (see below), general restrictions on the simple activity of lending money to others should not be restricted. In South Africa certain restrictions were removed with the result that there is no obstacle there in terms of alleviating poverty through microcredit.

Interest rate limitations: the Usury Act

A great strength of microcredit is that it has the possibility of covering its operational costs by charging interest on loans provided. Not only does this enable microcredit organizations to cover their costs but it moves those benefiting from services from a situation of dependence to that of being in control. The result is that organizations providing microcredit depend on their clients for survival and not the other way around. This ensures that organizations will do everything in their power to understand the needs of the poor, to understand the impact they are having and to provide the best service possible.

Beyond this, if an organization is able to cover its own costs then it moves away from reliance on donors and is not restricted by the availability of grant money to expand. The Holy Grail of microcredit is for organizations not only to cover their own costs but also to be able to convince commercial financial institutions, whether they be profit-maximizing or "socially responsible", that they are a sound investment. For this the microcredit organization must become profitable. The result would mean access to essentially unlimited amounts of capital or equity investment, which would allow great numbers of the poor to be reached with this vital service.

However, microcredit is expensive; it costs about as much to prepare and administer a US$50 loan as to do a US$5,000 loan. Thus worldwide institutions must charge rates that are considerably higher than the prime lending rate that they charge their best commercial customers. Rates of 15 per cent to 30 per cent above prime are common. In South Africa, due to the relative high salary burden that microcredit organizations must bear, such organizations charge between 45 per cent and 75 per cent above the prime rate.

In South Africa the Usury Act places limitations on the interest rate that may be charged on loans. In the early nineties an exemption from this act was introduced. This was extremely important and without it there could have been no legitimate microcredit activity in South Africa.

From 1994 to 1999 there was much debate about the Usury Act exemption owing to political worries about charging the poor a far higher interest rate than the rich pay for their finance. This debate was resolved by the creation of the Micro Finance Regulatory Council, the MFRC. All lenders who wish to use the Usury Act exemption must be registered with this council and must adhere to certain regulations such as publicizing their true interest rate. The MFRC also plays a consumer protection role in that it will follow up and investigate any complaints of lending malpractice from consumers.

But can the poor afford to pay a high rate of interest? All evidence from all parts of the world show that high interest rates are not a barrier for the poor. SEF itself does constant work in monitoring the impact of its loans on its clients. It has found that the impact is overwhelmingly positive and has found no evidence to suggest that its interest charge, 45 per cent above the current prime rate, is placing an unfair burden on clients.

Simply put: if the poor can pay these high, not exploitative, rates of interest then the service will be there for them and it will grow way beyond what donors and governments can support. If microcredit organizations are not allowed to charge these rates then there will be no service.

South Africa had an earlier debate concerning the Usury Act exemption, which was fuelled by the massive growth of a formal micro-lending industry that provided small cash loans to salaried people at rates in the region of 200 per cent-450 per cent above the prime rate. Within a few years, over a thousand such businesses were operating. Many hoped that the market would quickly ensure a drop in such rates, but this did not occur.

SEF has joined with those who are concerned about this industry and the exploitative rates charged. It is hoped that the Government will place a restriction on rates, such as a limit of ten times prime which was temporarily introduced but had to be revoked owing to a legal technicality.

Pro-active Steps

Creating a supportive environment

The new democracy in South Africa quickly identified the need to increase the access to credit for enterprise, especially for the previously disadvantaged. To this end it made efforts to create a supportive environment. This included the establishment of an apex facility to provide wholesale funds to microcredit organizations and an agency to provide non-financial support.

By its own admission the Government's strategy has produced very little. The apex facility has supported a number of initiatives, but it must carry a large part of the blame for the closure of many microcredit organizations in South Africa in the past year. In fact, this apex facility may have done more to shrink the access to microcredit than it has done to increase this access. The non-financial support agency has also been totally ineffective.

While the reasons for the failure of the South African Government efforts are complex, it is also clear that a considerable contributory factor has been pressure from the Government for speedy delivery. However, the microcredit sector in South Africa was very immature and the delivery agencies, principally NGOs, simply were not ready for the opportunity and challenge thrown to them by the Government. By trying to do too much too quickly, many organizations destroyed themselves.

Clearly a longer-term view, relying mainly on first building solid foundations or on maturing the sector, would have produced far better results. Such a strategy would probably have now seen the stage set for strong growth of microcredit and support services for small and medium microenterprises in South Africa.

In South Africa, as in experiences worldwide, the shortage of skills and experience among government agencies charged with funding or supporting the microcredit sector is a primary cause of their failure to carry out their mandate. A longer-term strategy is necessary, not only to build up a fledgling microcredit industry, but also to allow time for government agencies to build up their own competence. This is critical for a successful supportive intervention.

Bangladesh provides an exciting example of what can be achieved once the microcredit sector is mature. That country established an apex wholesale facility called Palli Karma-Sahayak Foundation (PKSF). It has financed over 400 NGOs and has been a major factor in developing the market in that country. Reasons given for the success of PKSF are (a) it was well protected from political pressure, and (b) Bangladesh was a country with a mature microcredit sector, with many strong microcredit organizations.

Where the microcredit sector in a country is not strong—and this applies to all but a handful of countries—then governments can be supportive by focusing on a long-term strategy, a ten to fifteen-year strategy, that aims firstly to ensure the strengthening of existing microcredit organizations, and secondly, to enable the creation of a sufficient number of new institutions, even though these may be small. Once the sector has reached a level of maturity that can sustain strong growth, large-scale delivery of services can be encouraged.

Preconditions for undertaking such a strategy include:

- Ensuring no political interference or politically driven delivery objectives;
- Recognizing that the support of microcredit takes very specific skills, requiring years of experience.

Therefore, the government must address this issue before embarking on implementation. This skills requirement will often mean that it will be more practical to establish such agencies on a regional as opposed to a national level.

Government funding of microcredit

Does this mean that government should stay out of any form of financing microcredit? Looking for a moment at SEF's experience, one can see that SEF has, since its inception, relied on government-funded wholesale facilities as the source of funds to borrow for onlending. Currently the organization is planning significant expansion and certainly hopes that the existing wholesale apex facility will again be the major source from which to borrow for onlending. Furthermore, SEF will approach the apex for the possibility of grant funding to subsidize the operational shortfall during this expansion. It should be noted that a key difference between this funding relationship and what has been previously described is that SEF is now a relatively mature organization and knows well what its limitations are. Thus it is in a strong position when it comes to agreeing to performance and growth expectations.

This illustrates the important role that government can play in funding microcredit. In fact in many developing countries, governments are more likely to be required to be the major funders of microcredit owing to the substantial absence of other funders such as the local private sector or international donors.

At the same time, while microcredit is recognized as a key strategy for overcoming poverty, more and more governments are ignoring microcredit, which they see as a private-sector initiative. Instead they focus on health and education issues. Microcredit is not a panacea, but where it is possible to combine it with health and education services, poverty alleviation becomes that much more effective. After all, microcredit ensures income, which leads to better quality food and better housing. How effective can health and education services be where children are insufficiently fed and housing is miserable?

At the same time, history has shown the world over that governments themselves are the most inappropriate institutions for the delivery of microcredit. Thus, direct intervention of this nature is certainly not being proposed.

Governments must, therefore, make funding available for the steady nurturing and development of their microcredit sectors and, as noted above, once these are well developed provide appropriate forms of funding to assist organizations to reach significant scale. In doing this, the preconditions noted in the previous section must be adhered to.

Government and postal banks

In South Africa, the Post Office and in particular its savings arm, the Postbank, provide an essential financial service, particularly in rural areas. The Postbank enables small-scale savings and money transfers, both vital services in the economic life of communities and vital for the poor in protecting themselves from financial shocks.

To date, the Government has ensured that the Postbank continues to deliver its financial services to the poor. However, it is now under pressure to become self-sustaining, and the Government's subsidies will be cut. There is, therefore, a danger that if the Government no longer provides a subsidy to the Postbank, it will be difficult for it to insist that these services are maintained.

Thus, it is recommended that where governments subsidize savings services, especially in rural areas, they must continue to do so until such time as existing financial institutions, such as postal savings facilities, are able to improve their operational efficiencies in order to be able to offer savings services on a profitable basis. Alternatively, governments must successfully facilitate the transfer over time of the same services in the same areas, (or preferably services that meet the needs of the poor even more effectively) to independent institutions.

4. Summary of policy recommendations

- Place no general restrictions on the simple activity of lending money.
- Allow lending at rates considerably higher than the prime lending rates of banks, but place a restriction of 75 per cent to 100 per cent above the prime lending rate.
- Create a supportive environment: if the microcredit sector in a country is not strong, then the government can focus on a ten- to fifteen-year strategy that aims firstly to strengthen existing microcredit organizations and secondly to enable the creation of a sufficient number of new institutions, even though these may be small. Once the sector has reached a level of maturity that can sustain strong growth, large-scale delivery of services can be encouraged.
- Ensure certain preconditions for undertaking such a strategy: no political interference; no politically driven delivery objectives; recognition that the support of microcredit takes very specific skills, requiring years of experience. This skills requirement will often mean that it will be more practical to establish such agencies on a regional as opposed to a national level. Therefore, governments must address those issues before embarking on implementation.

- Plan for government funding of microcredit: governments of developing countries must recognize that microcredit cannot be left up to the private sector and should give the same consideration to microcredit in their poverty alleviation strategy as they do to health, education and other services (under no circumstances should government consider being implementers of microcredit delivery). On the basis of the preconditions outlined above, governments must make funding available for the steady nurturing and development of their microcredit sectors, and once these are well developed, provide appropriate forms of funding to assist the organizations to reach significant scale.
- Government and savings facilities: where governments subsidize savings services, especially in rural areas, they must continue to do so until such time as existing financial institutions, such as postal banks, are able to improve their efficiencies to be able to offer savings services on a profitable basis, or until governments are successful in facilitating the transfer over time of the same services to independent institutions in the same areas (or preferably services that meet the needs of the poor even more effectively).

2

Financing for the poor and women: a policy critique

ZO RANDRIAMARO[1]

This paper addresses the question of financing for the poor and women in the particular context of financial liberalization in Africa. The first part highlights the key features of the economies of African countries and the problems these features pose for mobilizing resources for development, particularly in the context of women's economic activities. It explores the relevance of financial liberalization as a response to the challenges of financing for the poor and women. The second part underlines the problems of neo-liberal financial strategies in addressing the needs of micro- and small enterprises (MSEs), with a focus on their effects on women. The last part proposes alternative policy responses to those challenges.

1. Economic structure and challenges for financing

Economic structure and problems of resource mobilization

The issues related to financing for the poor and women in the context of financial liberalization are determined by the structural features of African economies. According to the Economic Commission for Africa (ECA), these include:

- predominance of subsistence and commercial activities;

---

[1] Manager, Gender and Economic Reforms in Africa (GERA) Programme, Third World Network—Africa. This paper has greatly benefited from the interaction with colleagues within and outside the GERA Programme. Special mention must be made of Tetteh Hormeku, for his comments and support.

- the narrow and disarticulated production base;
- lopsided development owing to the urban bias of public policies generally and development policies in particular;
- the open nature and the excessive external dependence of the economy, which have led to the disproportionate outflow of resources from African countries (ECA, 1996).

The consequences of the above structures for financial resources mobilization and allocation are that financing and financial instruments such as credit, insurance and banking are skewed in favor of the narrow import-export trade and cash-crop sectors. Similarly, imbalances exist between rural and urban areas, especially in terms of infrastructure and services.

The combined effects of these structural features for resource mobilization are manifold. Among others, they limit the scope of wealth creation within the African economies, as well as the levels of income and internal savings. Most importantly, the limited availability of resources for reinvestment in strategic sectors of the economy has come to mean that the most vulnerable operators, especially women, are the last on the list of access to financial resources.

Strategic responses: traditional versus neo-liberal financial strategies

Traditionally, the policies adopted for dealing with this situation supplemented non-market forms of financial support that were already targeted to what were regarded as strategic sectors of the economy, notably agriculture. With the adoption of free market policies since the 1980s and the liberalization of financial services, subsidized credit to the rural sector has been abandoned, along with government controls over interest rates, credit and capital flows, and institutional practices. It was assumed that the benefits from the expected expansion and diversification of the financial sector would be equally distributed among all the potential customers, including micro and small enterprises and women. Governments have also abandoned the long-term commitment to support those economic sectors whose development is crucial for sustainable economic growth and national development.

Most importantly, the general policy framework that has been developed under the pressure of the international financial institutions is distorted against the needs of those strategic sectors which are the mainstay of the poor and women in Africa. Indeed, related to this is the critical misconception that the main poverty problem has moved from the country-side to the burgeoning megacities of the developing world (IFAD, 2001). As underlined by the International Fund for Agricultural Development (IFAD) in February 2001, the global commitment to cutting poverty by 50 per cent by the year 2015 is bound to be unrealized because the world's rural poor have been marginalized. In terms of development assistance as well as domestic resource allocation, current policies are neglecting agriculture and fail to target the areas where the poor live, that is, mainly rural areas.

In keeping with the prevailing view among the international financial and development institutions that the private sector will be the engine of growth and that foreign investment is critical to overcoming poverty, the African countries have been urged to establish an enabling policy environment. A major distortion derives from the failure of the general policy framework that has been established in response to external requirements to recognize that in the case of Africa, growth is contingent upon the effective development of MSEs, which dominate the economic structure.

2. Neo-liberal financial strategies: limitations and problems

The measures that have been taken to liberalize the financial sector in Africa are based on the assumption that the private sector and the market will ensure an appropriate allocation of resources, including financial support to local production in strategic sectors of the economy such as agriculture.

However, the first question to be asked about financial liberalization is what liberalization means and whose interests it serves in the context of globalization. The main purpose of financial liberalization is first and foremost to attract foreign investment by putting an end to the so-called "financial repression". For most African countries, financial liberalization has been a selective process that has mainly served the interests of foreign capital. Many studies demonstrate that most of the MSEs have been initiated from the resources of their owners and not from credit provided by mainstream financial institutions (Nissanke, 1998; Dagra, 1998; Aryeetey, 1996). There is currently no friendly legal and socio-economic framework to support these MSEs, where women preponderate. In addition, a GERA study in Uganda found that the definition of the private sector used by the Government, donors and corporations excluded MSEs, thereby excluding small, poor producers, especially women (GERA Programme, 2000).

Besides, this assumption of the benefits of financial liberalization does not hold because it fails to take account of the very structure of African economies as they are described above. Indeed, in view of the relatively low level of profit generated and the high costs of operation, private financial institutions have no interest in reaching out to rural areas where MSEs preponderate.

Financial liberalization in Africa has generally taken place within an underdeveloped and inefficient financial sector, and in the context of a weak legal and regulatory framework. This has negatively affected the efficiency of financial intermediation and the incentives to save, and it has increased borrowing costs and the risk of bank failures (Mwalwanda, 2000).

These are major issues, since the large majority of the poorest people, including women, are involved in MSEs in rural areas, and depend on the agricultural sector for making their living (IFAD, 2001). There is therefore a real danger of further marginalization of the poor and women under the current poverty reduction strategies.

Failure to deliver

It is clear that the market-based mechanisms, which were supposed to allow a more varied and efficient intermediation between supply and demand, have not been able to address the needs of poor, small producers, especially women.

For the agricultural sector, except for the cash crop subsector, financial liberalization has resulted in the removal of any sort of provision of mainstream financial services. The search for profit is the major motivation, and rural credit is either provided according to commercial criteria or to special schemes isolated from mainstream finance.

The traditional subsector for food production has been particularly affected. Women play a crucial role in this subsector, which has generally been neglected in the allocation of productive resources, including public investment funds, and supporting institutions. Most of these resources, as well as the service sectors—banking, finance, transport, etc.,—are oriented towards the narrow and male-dominated import-export trade and cash crop subsectors. While women's crucial contribution to agricultural production is widely recognized, they suffer from the combined effects of these chronic imbalances against the food production subsector, gender-based constraints, and privatization and liberalization policies.

With regards to financial liberalization, the research carried out by the GERA Programme in Cameroon and other African countries found that financial sector reforms have not improved rural women's access to credit and financial services (GERA Programme, 2000). While the implications of financial liberalization for gender relations in many areas still need to be investigated, it is clear that because of the gendered nature of these markets, it cannot be assumed that men and women will benefit equally from measures to promote the development of financial markets.

Financing for women's economic activities: the microfinance ghetto

The gender-based constraints that prevent women from having access to and dealing with mainstream financial markets on equal conditions and terms with men are not taken into account. Too often, women have been subsumed in the category of the poor and vulnerable segments of society or the small savers and small borrowers, regardless of the peculiar and structural obstacles facing them, whereas these obstacles call for a special and differential treatment for women to ensure an equitable share of the potential benefits deriving from financial liberalization.

Other researchers have also underlined that the mainstream approach to women's access to credit and financial services overemphasizes microfinance, with the underlying assumption that it is the answer to the economic empowerment of women (UNIFEM, 2000). The direct implication is the containment of women's economic activity in the informal or small-scale sectors. Even as it is unanimously recognized that women rarely default on their loans, very few mechanisms have been set up to give them adequate credit to graduate from the informal and/or microlevel to the formal sector. According to the prevailing view, women are recipients or beneficiaries of donor microcredit programmes, but not creditworthy clients of mainstream financial markets. This is partly due to the fact that men are at the helm of decision-making in finance.

A more indirect implication is that public support to allow women to access the opportunities offered by the mainstream financial marketplace is not considered necessary. While there is an increasing recognition of the need to support microcredit programmes with the provision of social services, the underlying objective is still how to enable women to find, by themselves, their own ways to economic empowerment. Much of the literature on financial services for women also places great emphasis on the need for donors and governments to enact policies that encourage banks and other financial institutions to respond to women's demands and needs, rather than establish separate programmes. However, little has been done to fulfill women's right to get out of the ghetto of microfinance and to have equal access to mainstream financial services. When outreach services exist, the failure of governments to build infrastructure and/or to provide universal primary education are major obstacles affecting women's ability to benefit from those outreach services.

In addition, this overemphasis on microfinance has prevented its proponents, including many NGOs, from paying more attention to the fact that the interest rates applied in many microcredit schemes are basically set too high, mainly because women have no collateral and are therefore considered high-risk customers (Goma, 1999; UBINIG, 1999). It is also argued that be-cause women generally need small and short-term loans, high interest rates are required for handling the related transaction costs. Empirical evidence points to the fact that because of the pervasive poverty, women experience more and more pressures from their families to apply for microcredit. In some cases, these pressures have taken the form of violence against women.

Furthermore, while many donors and proponents of microfinance tend to make unjustified assertions about its "empowerment outcomes", there is very little evidence of such outcomes. In countries like India where the "self-help credit movement" has involved millions of women, rigorous studies have not documented actual changes in the income and expenditure patterns of the members of self-help groups (Menon-Sen, 2001).

All these are part of the context within which the actual impact of microfinance schemes on women's empowerment should be assessed. The cri-teria for such assessment should not be limited to the rate of loan repayment, the amount of savings and other quantitative criteria. The impact of microfinance schemes on social relations, and the extent to which they actu-ally contribute to reduce women's subordination are also key criteria.

3.   Options for an effective mobilization of financial resources for the poor and women

A new role of the State

There is an urgent need to assess financial liberalization and the related policies against their implications for the achievement of development objec-tives and equity, and not only against such criteria as gross domestic product, exports or budget deficit. An effective mobilization of financial resources for the poor and women calls for a new role of the State, which would go beyond withdrawing from its traditional role in finance and development, i.e., re-moval of controls, privatization and reduction of budget deficits, and aim at providing an innovative and supportive institutional framework for economic growth, sustainable and equitable human development.

This new role of the State would involve the adoption of financial policies and measures that do not reinforce the marginalization of small producers, in-cluding women, while enhancing private savings and supporting the domestic accumulation process. All these measures should be part of a network of finan-cial processes that are linked to the mainstream financial sector, in order to en-sure an effective and equitable access to financial resources. Because the availability of money alone does not create economic opportunities, enabling macroeconomic and market conditions for small producers and women's economic activity should also be promoted.

With regard to women and gender relations, what should be promoted is women's access to financial assets and savings instruments on appropriate and nondiscriminatory terms and conditions, especially as regards banking practices. Women's access to mainstream financial services should not be predicated on the prevailing view among financial institutions that women should change to fit bank requirements (GERA Programme, 2000). Reforms of banking policies and instruments are required to better serve women's demands and needs as clients of financial markets. Specifically, a recommendation from the GERA study in Uganda is to develop and implement an explicit financial policy that would increase the availability of capital to MSE sectors where women predominate (GERA Programme, 2000).

Rethinking the anti-poverty paradigm

Beyond these necessary policy actions, the mobilization of financial resources for the poor and women requires policy makers at all levels to address a more fundamental question about the current poverty reduction paradigm. In particular, the increasing tendency to identify the right to development of the poor and women with survival in the "global village" is a major issue.

Microfinance is an important coping mechanism for the poor and women, but it is not poverty's "magic bullet" (GERA Programme, 2000). Factors such as the hidden costs of microcredit and its limitations should be fully integrated in the assessment of its efficacy in terms of economic empowerment of the poor and women.

Furthermore, the overwhelming policy focus on the search for the best ways to enable the poor to meet their needs by themselves and through their own resources has led most policy makers to overlook the fundamental problem of inequities in redistribution both within and between countries. Just as in the case of women with microfinance, the poor seem to be trapped in a process of "ghettoization" with regard to the share of resources.

With respect to women and gender relations, policies should build on a sound analysis of the relationship between poverty reduction and gender equality, as evidence from various parts of the world shows that there is no linear relationship between gender equality and poverty reduction (Menon-Sen, 2001). Indeed, the analysis of the relationship between gender equality and poverty reduction has been obscured by critical misconceptions.

A major area of concern relates to conflating gender and poverty. Current strategies of poverty reduction seek to build on labour-intensive strategies, whereas the policy position needed for gender equality relates to labour-saving approaches. Concerns for efficiency seem to prevail at the expense of equity.

Another common assumption is that if the needs of the poor are addressed, since so many women are poor, gender equity will also be achieved. But first and foremost, the feminization of poverty means that poverty is a gendered experience. Gender issues are distinct from issues of poverty and class. As men's and women's experiences of poverty are different and mediated by social values and norms, poverty reduction strategies that are based on the assumption that the same policy instruments could address both poverty and gender inequalities may not improve the situation of women (GERA Programme, 2000).

The main lesson learned from the analysis of the issues related to financing for the poor and women is that poverty reduction and women's empowerment are contingent upon transforming the current economic model and development paradigm, as they are detrimental to the rights of women and the poor. Such an exercise is not only critical to the realization of their rights, but it would also be an opportunity to improve the effectiveness of poverty reduction programmes by including redistribution as a central element of their strategies.

References

Ajayi, S. I. (1997). An analysis of external debt and capital flight in the heavily indebted poor countries of sub-Saharan Africa. In *External Finance for Low-Income Countries,* Zubair Iqbal and Ravi Kanbur, eds. Washington, D.C.: International Monetary Fund.

Alemayehu, Geda (2000). Challenges and prospects for financing Africa's development. Draft background paper for Africa Knowledge Networks Forum Preparatory Workshop, 17-18 August 2000, United Nations Economic Commission for Africa, Addis Ababa, Ethiopia.

Amoako, K. Y. and G.A.A. Ali (1998). Financing development in Africa: some exploratory results. Nairobi: African Economic Research Consortium, Collaborative Project on Transition from Aid Dependency (mimeo).

Aryeetey, E. (1996). *The Complementary Role of Informal Financial Institutions in the Retailing of Credit : Evaluation of Innovative Approaches.* Technical Publication No. 58. Lagon, Ghana: University of Ghana, Institute for Statistical Social and Economic Research (ISSER).

Dagra, L. A. (1998). A comparative analysis of the accumulation process and capital mobilization in Mauritius, Tanzania and Zimbabwe. *African Development in a Comparative Perspective,* study No. 3, UNCTAD/GDS/MDPB/. Geneva: United Nations Conference on Trade and Development.

Economic Commission for Africa (1996). Cadre africain de référence pour les programmes d'ajustement structurel en vue du redressement et de la transformation socio-économique.

GERA Programme (2000). *Demanding Dignity: Women Confronting Economic Reforms in Africa*. Dzodzi Tsikata and Joanna Kerr, eds., with Cathy Blacklock and Jocelyne Laforce. Ottawa: The North-South Institute; and Accra: Third World Network—Africa.

Goma, Solange (1999). Background paper for the workshop on Gender Disaggregated Data. Sixth African Regional Conference on Women, 22-27 November 1999, Economic Commission for Africa, Addis Ababa, Ethiopia.

IFAD (2001). *Rural Poverty Report 2001: The Challenge of Ending Rural Poverty*. Rome: International Fund for Agricultural Development.

Ikhide, S.I. (1996). Commercial bank offices and the mobilization of private savings in selected sub-Saharan African countries. *The Journal of Development Studies*, vol. 3, No. 1.

Kaul, Inge (1999). *Towards a Paradigm of Embedded Financial Liberalization: Interlocking the Wheels of Private and Public Finance*. Policy Paper No. 13. Bonn: Development and Peace Foundation.

Menon-Sen, K. (2001). Gender, governance and the "feminization of poverty": the Indian experience. Paper presented at the OECD/DAC/WP – Gen and IAMWGE Joint workshop on Governance, Poverty Reduction and Gender Equality, Vienna, 23-25 April 2001.

Mwalwanda, C. T. (2000). Speaking notes at the African Knowledge Networks Forum Preparatory Workshop, Economic Commission for Africa. Addis Ababa, Ethiopia, 17-18 August 2000.

Nissanke, M. K. (1998). Financing enterprise development and export diversification in sub-Saharan Africa. In *African Development in a Comparative Perspective*, study No. 8, UNCTAD/GDS/MDPB/. Geneva: United Nations Conference on Trade and Development.

Singh, A, and A. Zammit (2000). International capital flows: identifying the gender dimension. *World Development*, vol. 28, No.7.

UBINIG Policy Research Group for Development Alternatives (1999). Cited in the report of the Third World Network Workshop on Economic Crisis, Social Consequences and People's Responses, Manila, 9-11 August 1999.

United Nations Development Fund for Women, 2000. *Progress of the World's Women 2000*, New York: United Nations.

3

A social role for foreign banks in poor countries

HANNS MICHAEL HOELZ[1]

This chapter concerns the positive social role that foreign banks can play in developing countries based on the experience of Deutsche Bank.

As an institution with offices in 70 countries and activities around the world, Deutsche Bank recognizes the importance of the developing world to both our current and future success. We recognize, however, that our vision and plans must also include a long-term investment in the social development of new markets. As such we recognize the importance of an enduring "third sector" and the obligations of corporations to facilitate the development of local capacity and viable civil society organizations.

1. Corporate citizenship

Corporations enjoy many of the same rights and privileges as other members of a community. Like any citizen, this membership includes responsibilities as well. Deutsche Bank believes that the realities of globalization offer a unique opportunity to effect positive change, encourage sustainable communities and develop stable societies.

Moreover, we recognize that this commitment cannot be a financial one alone. Building a common culture of concern and responsiveness among our employees is essential to our corporate citizenship strategy. A broad variety of backgrounds, talents, cultures and abilities makes Deutsche Bank a successful financial organization. These are the same strengths that we call upon to address the needs of the communities in which we operate and beyond.

---

[1]   Head of Global Public Affairs, Deutsche Bank, Germany.

We believe our role in society must be one that helps buffer the impact of change on those most vulnerable. We also seek to encourage those most able to utilize the momentum of change to define a future of enlightenment, justice and prosperity. Many of the programmes I will refer to are quite new. As we react to our changing world, we learn every day how to adapt what we are doing. Our commitment is a work in progress, but it is evolving constantly as we seek a new understanding of the way in which business can interact positively with society. It is through this effort that we strive towards our goal of being both a global corporation and a global citizen.

Let us consider the concept of corporate citizenship itself. It is a relatively new term that has for many replaced the word philanthropy. Not too long ago, a reporter asked me what the difference was. After pausing for a moment to consider, I explained to him very carefully that there had been a change in the use of words because there had been a change in the meaning. Often philanthropy connotes little more than providing funds, simply giving money in response to a crisis and human suffering. We, however, choose to use our position in society to bring about positive change beyond what simple financial contributions can accomplish in the short term. The first step in doing this is to ask oneself what it means to be "global".

Deutsche Bank has offices in nearly 70 countries, industrialized, emerging and developing. We employ people who are citizens of those countries, residents of those communities who have families in those cities and towns. Corporate citizenship for us is about them and their neighbours. One cannot make a difference without fully participating in the life of the communities in which we operate. By being present, making a long-term commitment to make a positive difference, by being a partner on whom people can count, can trust—that is corporate citizenship.

Deutsche Bank's corporate citizenship activities, with their origins in Germany, have a long and proud history. With our emergence as an international corporation with a presence in diverse markets throughout the world, we call upon this tradition to define a new corporation that acknowledges its responsibilities as a truly global corporate citizen.

The implications of globalization for the goal of sustainable development should be of paramount importance to those of us who work within the financial services industry. While our companies are faced with enormous challenges to compete successfully in the new global marketplace, none of us would deny that globalization is essentially a force of opportunity for multinational corporations as old boundaries fall to the wayside, capital sources flow more freely and new markets open. This momentum of growth cannot be sustained, however, unless we work to ensure that globalization results in broad benefits for the majority of the world's people and especially for those living outside the economic mainstream. Not only is this a moral imperative, but a necessary one as well. In the short term it is certainly in our own interest to work to counter the mounting, and well-organized, grass-roots backlash against globalization. In the long term, perhaps the most compelling argument for our involvement is our own survival. To maintain the economic growth that fuels the expansion and growth of our businesses we must remove the barriers of poverty and ignorance that isolate much of the world's people from the marketplace and impede their access to economic independence and prosperity.

According to the World Bank, today 3 billion people, nearly half of the world's population, live on less that US$2 per day; 1.3 billion live on less than US$1 per day. The average income in the richest 20 countries is now 37 times that of the poorest 20 countries, a gap that has doubled in the past 40 years. These facts are a great concern to all of us.

2. Microfinance

Deutsche Bank employs an explicit strategy to promote sustainable communities through the strategic deployment of capital as a tool to reach disadvantaged communities and populations with opportunities to enter the economic mainstream. Support of microfinance is part of that strategy.

In a large number of developing and emerging markets, the financial services that citizens of industrialized nations take for granted are often available only to an elite group of individuals. With poorly developed laws regarding property rights, low levels of literacy and extremely limited income, the vast majority of persons living in many developing nations cannot acquire simple credit for lack of collateral or access to a lending institution. Making available to these communities the basic resources needed for economic progress would break the cycle and very much accelerate the alleviation of poverty, an essential tool of development.

By bringing the potential of capital to communities that would otherwise not have access, we open up the possibility for them to take advantage of their own creativity, ingenuity, hard work and spirit. In this capacity Deutsche Bank, in partnership with local institutions, can play a most purposeful role in creating a climate of enthusiasm and trust.

The promise of microfinance to alleviate poverty and generate economic growth through the provision of small credits to emerging entrepreneurs can succeed only if programmes move to scale and operational self-sufficiency.

With this as a goal we established the Deutsche Bank Microcredit Development Fund (DB MDF) with the sole purpose of providing subordinated debt to local microfinance programmes that can serve as collateral in leveraging local domestic bank borrowings.[2] It is our belief that establishing conventional relationships with domestic commercial banks is an essential step to freeing microfinance programmes from their dependency on donor aid. In addition to monies from Deutsche Bank itself, our Fund is capitalized through donations from high-net worth clients of our private bank, providing them with an opportunity to leverage their philanthropic resources to achieve a reach and scale of involvement that alone they could not achieve. DB MDF loans to microfinance programmes are low interest loans with terms as long as eight years, and this "patient capital" can generate at least two to one leverage in borrowings from a local bank. The Deutsche Bank offices throughout the world help find good programmes to support and can play the important role of nurturing relationships between microfinance organizations and local banks. Presently DB MDF has loans in place supporting microfinance programmes in Bosnia and Herzegovina, Chile, Colombia, India, Mexico, Pakistan, the Russian Federation and South Africa.

Deutsche Bank is exploring ways to broaden its involvement in microfinance and we are looking at other capital market roles we can play as well. We can help to train microfinance management and encourage hospitable regulatory environments in which to nurture the growth of programmes throughout the developing world.

All of our activities are premised on strong operating partnerships with organizations that can complement Deutsche Bank's own capacity and resources. It has been enormously helpful to us to work with Grameen Bank, Women's World Bank and ACCION International, as microfinance intermediaries that can introduce us to local programmes that meet their high standards for performance. We also benefit from strong relationships with the Consultative Group to Assist the Poorest (CGAP), the United Nations Development Programme (UNDP) and the International Fund for Agricultural Development (IFAD). We support the Microcredit Summit as well and work collaboratively with donors, microfinance practitioners and governments to reach the goal of providing microfinance to 100 million of the poor, especially women, by 2005. Certainly the goals of sustainable development, whether in addressing environmental issues or poverty alleviation strategies, can best be

---

[2]   Subordinated debt has some equity-like characteristics (e.g., in the event of bankruptcy, claims of holders of subordinated debt are treated after those of conventional creditors). Equity in a firm (and subordinated debt) can be pledged as collateral for a loan — Eds.

served when we reach across the boundaries of sectors and create new partnerships among non-governmental organizations, governments, donor agencies and other corporations.

3. Sustainable development

Whereas poverty alleviation is necessary to ensure sustainable development, our commitment to sustainability does not end with microfinance. Deutsche Bank, both internally and externally, is committed to following a path of sustainable development.

In Germany, Deutsche Bank received its ISO14001 (Environmental Management System) certification in May of 1999. Environmental factors are always included in our credit risk policy, and we have set up a team to help our small and medium-size clients perform environmental risk assessments and then help them design solutions when problems arise. In addition to this we have added photovoltaic cells and rainwater collection devices to some of our buildings. We are striving to improve our energy, water and waste efficiency. We are also actively working to increase awareness of this important issue among our own colleagues.

Sustainable development is a global issue, and one that cannot be tackled by any one corporation, or even one nation alone. Thus, we realize how important our network of partners is in this effort. We are active members of the World Business Council for Sustainable Development, the United Nations Environmental Programme Financial Services Initiative, the Bellagio Forum for Sustainable Development and the World Bank Protoype Carbon Fund. We were very proud to be invited by the Secretary-General of the United Nations, Kofi Annan, to be among the first organizations to be a part of the Global Compact, where we have made efforts to highlight our record not only on the environment, but also in the areas of human rights and labour.

Through these important organizations, we share best-practice policy and are able to pool our resources to make important contributions to the multifaceted and developing issues that have come to be known as sustainable development.

At Deutsche Bank, we believe that a commitment to society must be long-term. Simply donating money to programmes may be helpful as a temporary support, but the fundamental structures and support mechanisms that must be built to ensure continuity and real change can only come about through consistency, reliability and trust—in short—real partnership.

4. Think global, act local

For us, much of our corporate citizenship commitment is a local issue. Globalization has meant that companies are active in more places with greater reach and larger resources. However, globalization is not synonymous with centralization. A person in Frankfurt cannot know and understand the needs of a community in Africa, Asia or in South America. Thus, globalization affords us the opportunity to have individuals, who work for the Bank but live in diverse communities, take our central ideas and coordination and implement them in the most effective way for the communities of which they are a part.

Deutsche Bank has individuals and resources dedicated to corporate citizenship located in America, Europe and Asia and the Pacific, and we are in the process of establishing a foundation in Africa. Through central coordination, we can all chose to dedicate our energies to a specific issue, such as education, in all of these diverse regions. The approach taken in Mexico may not be the same as in India, but the outcome, a better educated population more prepared to succeed in the modern world, is nevertheless the same.

This is our philosophy: "Think global, act local". Emerging markets require different methods and approaches. The issues, however, are often not fundamentally different. Education is a necessity for prosperity, regardless of the level. The message must be tailored to meet the needs of each region. The partners must be carefully chosen and the dedication must be real and long-term. Thus, we have a worldwide corporate citizenship commitment that proudly bears the signature of Deutsche Bank, which at the same time is implemented by local individuals with local roots in their own communities. We are dedicated to making a difference and do not hesitate to be innovative. Most importantly, we recognize the importance of listening to our neighbours and learning from our colleagues, our friends and our partners.

4

Stripping structural adjustment programmes of their poverty-reduction clothing

DOUGLAS HELLINGER, WITH KAREN HANSEN-KUHN AND APRIL FEHLING[1]

For over two decades, through their protest and critiques, citizens around the globe have consistently and overwhelmingly rejected the domestic manifestation of global economic management, namely the structural adjustment programmes conceived by the Bretton Woods institutions and major donor governments, as well as the global and regional trade accords that complement those programmes.

These programmes have embodied an unprecedented intervention in the economic affairs of sovereign States. In our view, it has undermined democratic processes by forcing even representative governments to respond first and foremost to the policy demands and financial interests of their creditors rather than to the needs and priorities of their own citizens. Ultimately, it has limited choice to only one economic approach, which, not surprisingly, has not generated development. To the contrary, everything predicted in terms of the failure of the development process by the critics of adjustment—who were consistently dismissed by the international financial institutions (IFIs) as misguided—has come to pass. Local businesses and farms have been destroyed. Employment and incomes have been slashed. Poverty and economic inequality have sharply increased. Greater pressure has been placed on women and on ecological resources. And social, economic and financial instability have been generated.

---

[1]   The Development Group for Alternative Policies (The Development GAP), Washington, D.C.

For two decades, Southern governments seem to us to have been unable to challenge economic orthodoxy without retribution, and most Northern governments have also chosen to remain silent on these issues. Civil society has filled the void and championed not only resistance to the structural adjustment paradigm but also an increasingly articulated vision for change. Started as a backlash against the destruction of local livelihoods and communities, this citizen challenge has grown into a global movement that is beginning to change the political, if not quite yet the economic, landscape. The movement calls for convergence around a particular set of values and principles, namely respect for diversity, equity, self-reliance, self-determination, community and environmental sustainability, democratic economic decision-making, transparency and accountability.

Given the resistance to these external pressures by transnational companies, by a new Southern economic and financial elite, and, most importantly, by the finance ministries of the Group of 7, this change will not be easy nor without costs. In our view, it will continue to be met with repression and obfuscation, and the speed and direction of change that does take place will not necessarily reflect the often desperate needs of a broad array of population groups and economic sectors. What is required, therefore, is the forging of partnerships between civil-society movements and other parties, including official international institutions, that can clear paths for meaningful change.

We are at a particular moment in the historical process of change, a moment when the failures and crises of corporate-led globalization and the mobilization of citizens worldwide in defense of their rights and livelihoods are outstripping the slow and marginal reforms in global economic management. The challenge is for official institutions to get out ahead of the curve, to join civil society in changing the nature of global decision-making and to avoid being swept along in the current confluence of shortsighted self-interest that history will undoubtedly judge harshly.

To the IFIs, we echo the demands of millions of people around the globe when we say that it is well past time to put an end to the destructive practice of imposing corporate-engendered economic policies on client countries. To the World Bank, in particular, we say that it is far from sufficient to develop so-called poverty programmes limited to social considerations. We believe it is now generally accepted across civil society and within many Governments and official institutions that the Bank's own economic adjustment programmes are not only undemocratic and have failed to achieve their stated objectives, but have themselves contributed significantly to the growing poverty and inequalityand to the destruction of local economies. Indeed, theextremely rigid economic policy framework in which the IFIs have been caught makes it extremely difficult, if not impossible, for their leaders to do the kind of work they say they want to do in support of meaningful development.

Five years ago, the President of the World Bank, James Wolfensohn, accepted a challenge from NGOs and requested the establishment of a mechanism for jointly assessing with civil society the domestic impact of these adjustment programmes. That mechanism, which became known as the Structural Adjustment Participatory Review Initiative (SAPRI), has included extensive processes of broad citizen mobilization, structured consultations and participatory research in a number of countries on four continents. The civil-society side of the assessment has been coordinated by the global civil-society network, "SAPRIN", for which the Development GAP serves as Secretariat. The highly inclusive, democratic and grassroots nature of civil-society participation in the Initiative, along with the World Bank's intimate involvement and the financial support from European Governments, the European Union, the United Nations Development Programme and other prominent institutions, has given SAPRI and its emerging findings a high level of credibility.

These findings substantiate the depth of many of the problems that have been at the root of public protest. Labour-market reforms have undermined workers' rights, security and incomes. The resultant decline in local demand, along with policies of precipitous import liberalization and tight credit, has contributed significantly to the destruction of much of the small and medium-scale productive sector in these countries and of the millions of jobs these enterprises and farms provide around the world. The privatization of public utilities has often made affordable services unavailable to poor and working people. Public-expenditure reform and cost-recovery requirements have also put health care and education out of the reach of a growing number of people.

Recognizing the broadening and deepening of poverty around the world under the economic adjustment programmes of the past two decades and the broadening critique, the IFIs have recently sought to address this tragedy through a more explicit focus on poverty. Now, in order to qualify for official debt reduction and future credits, and under the guidance of the Bank and the International Monetary Fund (IMF), the Governments of low-income countries must develop Poverty Reduction Strategy Papers (PRSPs) in consultation with civil society organizations.

1. Our critique of the PRSPs

The PRSPs of today, like all previous IFI proposals and programmes to address poverty, have a fatal weakness. It is our view that because governments have to respond to their official creditors rather than to their own citizens, they leave structural adjustment programmes firmly in place to continue to eat away at the livelihoods of poor and working people. By engaging civil-society organizations under the banner of popular participation, but then ignoring their key input regarding adjustment programmes, the IFIs not only breed further cynicism in civil society, they also rob the assessments of fundamental knowledge and critical perspectives and experiences, and ensure that these analytical instruments will prove useless in attaining their stated goals.

The fact that structural adjustment policies can be found today dressed in PRSP clothing can be gleaned from a review of recent interim and final PRSPs of individual countries and their juxtaposition with citizen analysis of the impact of adjustment policies in the respective countries. We cite a few examples below.

Bolivia

Bolivia was one of the first countries to undertake a structural adjustment process. In late 1985, the Government began to implement, with the assistance of IMF and the World Bank, an adjustment programme known as the New Economic Policy, or Law 21060. That programme, and the programmes funded since then, have emphasized trade liberalization, export promotion, privatization, reductions in State subsidies, and the elimination of numerous labour laws.

The emphasis on export production, combined with trade liberalization, has contributed significantly to poverty in the rural sector. Small-scale farmers, who comprise 40 per cent of the population and produce 70 per cent of the country's agricultural output, have been largely excluded from the push for non-traditional exports, with most of the available credit and investment capital in the sector going to agribusiness firms producing for export. Farmers who continue to produce for the domestic market have been further hurt by the lowering of trade barriers. Hence, beginning with the privatization and closures of mines in 1985 when the adjustment programme began, there has been a significant increase in migration to the cities and to the coca-producing Chapare region.

Meanwhile, in the urban sector, official unemployment figures dropped a bit during the 1990s, only to increase dramatically in the past two years to reach 30-year highs for the country. Most of the employment creation that has taken place has been in precarious low-wage, low-productivity, informal-sector jobs. According to data from the Economic Commission for Latin America and the Caribbean, the percentage of workers in such jobs increased from 62.5 percent in 1989 to 65.5 percent in 1997, while average incomes in that sector decreased during the same period. This increase in informal-sector activity has occurred in large part because of the bankruptcy of larger productive enterprises. The investment and trade-liberalization policies pushed under the adjustment programmes have made the Bolivian economy extremely vulnerable to changes in the global economy. Bolivian textile companies estimate, for example, that over 300 small enterprises producing cotton shirts closed recently due to a sudden surge of cheap imports from Brazil, and even medium-sized and large-scale businesses have been forced to cut production and jobs (see ECLAC, 1999, pp. 263-265; Campos, 1999).

Public frustration over the adjustment programmes reached the breaking point with the planned privatization of water utilities in Cochabamba. When the Bolivian Government sold the city water system to a consortium of foreign investors, the resulting rates for residents were three times higher than those they had previously paid. A general strike that closed the city down for four days was followed a few months later by massive protests over this and other government policies and by numerous deaths.

While Bolivia's PRSP does not deal with the privatization issue or a number of others raised by citizens in the consultative process, it does reference some civil-society concerns, including some raised by Jubilee 2000 in its own, separate consultation. For example, attention is given to the need to increase access by small producers to credit and technical assistance, and there is even a section describing the vulnerability of the Bolivian economy to external shocks and natural disasters. According to the PRSP, per capita gross domestic product (GDP) fell 1.7 percent in 1999-2000 as a result of these shocks, Bolivia's terms of trade fell almost 40 percent in the 1990s, and the Government and international institutions have projected continued deterioration in the near future (see Bolivia, 2001).

However, there is a curious disconnect in the document between the recognized impacts of the adjustment programme, particularly the trade-liberalization and export-promotion policies, and the policy recommendations. In the end, there is minimal priority given to microfinance development, and no thought given to restructuring an economic strategy based on exports of natural resources and primary commodities in light of the country's increased economic vulnerability. The Government only recommends, in other documents, the establishment of an emergency employment programme to ameliorate the impact of shocks.

The reason for not dealing with fundamental economic causes of poverty is clear: according to World Bank and IMF documents and statements, the macroeconomic targets previously agreed to by the Bolivian Government are not open to negotiation (*Actualidad Económica*, 21 May 2000). Any contradicting recommendations developed in the PRSPs would be subordinated to the macroeconomic reforms. In fact, the PRSP emphasizes that poverty reduction will result from a long-term growth rate of five per cent, despite the fact that current projections are no higher than three per cent and as low as 1.5 per cent and that recent, adjustment-related policies have generated increased inequalities and poverty (Eurodad, 2001).

Burkina Faso

Under Burkina Faso's trade-liberalization programme, the dismantling of tariffs has resulted in a rapid influx of imported goods, which have increased some 26 per cent since 1998 (Burkina Faso, 2000a, p.3). The Policy Framework Paper for drawings by Burkina Faso from the Enhanced Structural Adjustment Facility of IMF in 2000-2002 acknowledged that the country's external position had deteriorated "primarily on account of a rapid rise in imports," resulting in a chronic balance-of payments deficit (Burkina Faso, 1999, p.2) [2]. At the same time, the removal of protection for local industry left small Burkinabè firms unable to compete with imported goods from abroad. But, rather than promote the development of local industry, the Bank and the Fund have emphasized that "agriculture and other primary sector activities will continue to be the main source of growth" and revenue (Ibid., p. 3).

Meanwhile, the reliance on primary commodity exports has left Burkina Faso highly vulnerable to fluctuations in commodity prices and natural disasters. Poor farmers have borne the brunt of this vulnerability. Burkina Faso's 17 April 2000 Letter of Intent to the IMF, which embodies its policy commitments, reports that not only has the percentage of poor people in the country increased, but that the incidence of poverty is highest among farmers, particularly those growing cash crops (Burkina Faso, 2000a). Thus, rather than

---

[2]   Before adoption of the policy on poverty reduction strategies in 1999, IMF concessional lending to poor countries required approval by the borrowing government and the respective executive boards of a joint International MonetaryFund/World Bank Policy Framework Paper. Concessional loans were provided through the Enhanced Structural Adjustment Facility (ESAF), since renamed the Poverty Reduction and Growth Facility (PRGF) — Eds.

improving macroeconomic indicators and the economic situation of the people of Burkina Faso, the emphasis on primary-commodity exports has eroded the country's attempts to achieve economic stability and increased, rather than decreased, poverty.

To make matters worse, one of the aims of the privatization process in Burkina Faso has been the complete withdrawal of the State from agricultural production and marketing, and supply of inputs and credit (Burkina Faso, 1999, para. 30). Implementing this policy has created serious problems for the country's small farmers, who make up 97.5 per cent of cotton producers and produce some 70 per cent of the nation's cotton. Privatization has pushed the cost of inputs such as fertilizers out of the reach of most farmers, and private investors have shown little interest in entering the sector. Since the privatization of the State-owned cotton production and marketing company, farmers have been required to transport their seed cotton to collection centres, thus reducing the costs incurred by the marketing company. This has created a new barrier and a significant new cost for the vast majority of cotton farmers who are poor.

None of this analysis is found in the country's PRSP, whose primary emphasis is the acceleration of growth rates. Maintaining macroeconomic stability and improving the competitiveness of the economy are listed as key elements in the achievement of that objective. In one of the world's poorest countries, where poverty is actually growing, the PRSP calls for lowering the minimum wage and reducing benefits paid by formal-sector employers as part of a strategy to reduce production costs (Burkina Faso, 2000, p. 48).

In its description of the determinants of rural poverty, the PRSP lists the low productivity of agricultural activities (caused by low levels of education and the lack of technical assistance), as well as sharp fluctuations in the prices offered for agricultural goods and the lack of marketing channels for those goods. The solutions listed later in the paper, however, fail to address these problems. The paper recommends that the Government should disengage itself from remaining production and marketing activities, suggesting instead the strengthening of private-sector provision of technical assistance and increasing competition among private-sector distribution channels. While the PRSP recommends strengthening the Government's "support and advisory role vis-à-vis private operators" (Burkina Faso, 2000, p. 50), there is no mention of how the poorest farmers would afford such privately provided services, how they would avoid being exploited by private traders, or how they would reduce farmers' vulnerability to price fluctuations.

Mozambique

In Mozambique, in the face of desperate poverty and unemployment, the IMF and the World Bank pressed the Government to focus on controlling inflation, in part through monetary restraint. Between 1990 and 1995, available credit fell by two thirds as a result of tight monetary policy (Hanlon, 1996, p. 17). Small and medium-scale businesses report that access to credit continued to be one of their biggest problems. Finance Minister Salomão denounced the Fund's obsession with inflation targets, saying, "Any adjustment programme that does not generate results on the side of production is a failed programme...We might reach a situation where there is nothing to adjust anymore" (Fauvet, 2000, p.18).

Most Mozambican cashew processing firms have closed since 1997, leaving some 8,500 people unemployed. The Bank and the Fund had insisted that producers would be better off selling their crops for export. In 2000, the prices paid to producers dropped to less than half those paid in 1999, and, as the cashew market in India dried up, it was unclear whether Mozambican producers would be able to sell their crops at all (Mozambique News Agency, 2000). Meanwhile, the emphasis on export crops led to decreased production of food crops, particularly during the early 1990s.

Since 1987, the combined impact of the nation's privatization programme and its trade-liberalization process has been the loss of some 116,000 jobs. Estavoa Mabumu, head of international affairs for the Mozambican Workers' Organization, the country's main labour federation, explained at the end of 2000 that only 20 percent of the people who lost their jobs had found alternative employment (United Nations, 2000).

According to IMF statistics, GDP growth in Mozambique averaged 8 percent a year during the second half of the 1990s (IMF, 2001, p. 67) and the country's Interim PRSP places strong emphasis on the continuance of economic growth in order to achieve poverty reduction. The document also states that macroeconomic policy would be carried out in accord with the 1999-2000 Policy Framework Paper negotiated with the IMF. Such policies, however, have not benefited the majority of the population of Mozambique, and while the Interim PRSP outlines proposed measures on health, education and rural infrastructure, it fails to address the problems resulting from the current adjustment programme and the programme's contribution to poverty and income inequality (Mozambique, 2000).

United Republic of Tanzania

Adjustment reforms have liberalized trade in the United Republic of Tanzania, encouraging imports and export growth. Restrictions on imports have been lifted, export taxes have gradually been eliminated, and tariff rates have been reduced. Manufacturing has declined, however, as trade has been liberalized, with manufactured exports deteriorating sharply (IMF, 2000, p. 24). A flood of sugar imports has damaged the Tanzanian sugar industry. The decline of local industry has been a significant contributing factor to the fall in formal-sector employment from 9.2 percent of the labour force in 1990 to 8.1 percent in 1995 (van der Hoeven, 2000).

Tanzania's new financial regime has also contributed to significant declines in borrowing and investment by farmers and industry. In order to comply with adjustment demands and reduce inflation, the Government has enforced a tight monetary policy—restricting the money supply and raising interest rates—and sharply curtailed fiscal expenditures throughout the 1990s. High collateral requirements and minimum loan amounts of private commercial banks have also made borrowing almost impossible for small farmers and businesspeople. Credit to domestic borrowers declined by more than half between 1990 and 1998, while the majority of the decreased lending for agricultural production has gone to large-scale rather than small-scale farmers (World Bank, 1996, p. 7). Coffee producers today lack the capital for large replanting schemes, and private buyers have been reluctant to assist farmers in planting new trees (Wallengren, 1997, p. 18). Manufacturers in the food-processing sector, which the World Bank claims is crucial to higher economic growth, have also been unable to secure financing to invest in modern technology and costly inputs (African News Service, 2000). Not surprisingly, participants in both the Bank's participatory poverty assessments and the PRSP Zonal Workshops identified limited access to credit to finance inputs and technology as one of the most important constraints to production (Tanzania, 2000, p. 11; World Bank, 1996, p. 86).

Hence, NGOs and other civil-society groups in Tanzania have strongly contested the country's adjustment programme and are particularly disturbed by what is *not* included in its PRSP. While the programme has coincided with deteriorating quality-of-life indicators, an eroding industrial base, increasing unemployment, instability and income inequality, none of the adjustment-related issues raised by citizens' groups were adequately addressed in either the interim or final PRSP. Furthermore, not only did the IMF, the World Bank and the Government negotiate required policy conditions in closed meetings, but these reform measures are not disclosed in the final PRSP document (Cheru, 2001, p. 14).

There are no proposed policies in the document that would directly enhance access by the productive sector to credit. The only measure recommended that might help farmers' access in this regard is a proposal for land to be registered and made available as collateral for loans, a policy that would likely lead to farmers losing their land in the absence of other support and access to marketing channels. Meanwhile, rather than making proposals to deal with the country's decreasing food security and growing malnutrition, the PRSP supports further development of cash crops for export. Furthermore, in spite of the negative impact of trade liberalization on local enterprises and jobs, the detailed and still operative policy matrix from the Interim PRSP calls for "simplifying the tariff structure and reducing protection."[3]

2. What is required

In our view, the leaders of the specialized United Nations agencies have a responsibility to distance themselves from the PRSP process and to help attack today's burgeoning and pernicious global poverty at its roots. Rather than accept the structural adjustment agenda in the PRSPs, the United Nations system can and should launch parallel processes that look specifically at the poverty effects of adjustment programmes. Twenty years ago, the proponents of what became known as the "Washington Consensus" cited the economic-policy environment as a much more powerful factor in the development process than development projects and investments. It is therefore logical and necessary to examine how the policies that emerged from the much heralded "policy dialogue" have played out in the lives of the people, families and communities of the South.

In helping the United Nations system finance these national exercises, forward-thinking Northern governments would not only be underwriting critical and objective analysis that is missing in the flawed PRSP processes, they would also be significantly strengthening the role of UN agencies in promoting equitable economic and social development. Involvement in such an exercise, in conjunction with civil-society organizations and interested parties in government in the countries in which they work, would establish the United Nations as a focal point in the endeavour to achieve economic justice and would help establish a strong platform for further action in this area. Civil society movements, including SAPRIN, which have been constructing this

---

[3]   A footnote in the final PRSP states that the policy matrix from the Interim PRSP provides details of the reform programme being implemented (see Tanzania 2000, pp. 17-18 and 2000a, Appendix III). The Logical Frame attached to the final PRSP is much more general and less descriptive than the policy matrix (see Tanzania, 2000, Annex II).

platform over the past decade, would embrace a UN leadership role in articulating a new convergence around development approaches that are more just, sustainable and locally determined.

The parameters of this new convergence have been set by civil society around a set of principles that translate into a development agenda featuring strong domestic productive sectors, food self-sufficiency, national economic integration, rising and equitable family incomes, savings and purchasing power, and a reduced dependence on external assistance and borrowing. How such expanding, equitable and sustainable economies are achieved can best be left to each government and its citizenry to determine. Targets can be set internationally and democratically, and international financing can be linked to progress in these target areas.

The new convergence requires a coming together of various parties with similar values, interests and goals. More specifically, it calls for concrete collaboration among and between various UN agencies, civil-society movements and organizations, and principled and emboldened governments and ministries in the countries of the South and North, as well as the assistance of economists with links to local realities. Within the United Nations itself, it will require cooperation among the leaders of its various agencies rooted in a common vision of, and commitment to, progressive and democratic social change. To join civil society in the expansion of a new public platform and convergence on the issue of economic policy entails risk, but this risk pales in comparison with the sacrifice that millions of people have made over the past generation. As the march of history unfolds in the streets of Cochabamba, Washington, Seoul and Prague, what is now needed is for people of good faith in officialdom to speak out against the failure and injustice of the current economic system and to shift their institutions firmly in a different direction.

References

Africa News Service (2000). "Agro-processing: the giant sleeping industry in Tanzania," 1 August.

Bolivia, Government of (2001). *Republic of Bolivia: Poverty Reduction Strategy Paper – PRSP.* La Paz, March (available on the Internet at www.imf.org/external/country/bol/index.htm).

Burkina Faso, Ministry of Economy and Finance (2000). *Burkina Faso: Poverty Reduction Strategy Paper.* Ouagadougou, 25 May (available on the Internet at www.imf.org/external/country/bfa/index.htm).

_____ (2000a). Letter of Intent and Memorandum on Economic and Financial Policies for 2000. Ouagadougou, 17 April (available on the Internet at www.imf.org/external/country/bfa/index.htm).

Burkina Faso, Government of, in collaboration with the staffs of the International Monetary Fund and the World Bank (1999). *Burkina Faso: Enhanced Structural Adjustment Facility Policy Framework Paper, 2000-2002.* Ouagadougou, 2 August (available on the Internet at www.imf.org/external/country/bfa/index.htm).

Campos, Alejandro (1999). "Textiles reeling from Brazilian debacle." Inter Press Service (10 March).

Cheru, Fantu (2001). "The Highly Indebted Poor Countries (HIPC) Initiative: a human rights assessment of the Poverty Reduction Strategy Papers (PRSP)." Report submitted by the independent expert on the effects of structural adjustment policies and foreign debt on the full enjoyment of all human rights, particularly economic, social and cultural rights. United Nations Commission on Human Rights, Fifty-seventh session (E/CN.4/2001/56).

Economic Commission for Latin American and the Caribbean of the United Nations (ECLAC, 1999). "Annexo estadístico." In *Panorama Social de América Latina, 1998.* Santiago de Chile.

European Network on Debt and Development (Eurodad, 2001). "English translation of the Bolivian CSO position on the PRSP." Brussels, 22 May.

Fauvet, Paul (2000). "Mozambique: growth with poverty." *Africa Recovery,* vol. 14, No. 3 (October).

van der Hoeven, Rolph (2000). "Poverty and structural adjustment: some remarks on trade-offs between equity and growth." Employment Paper 2000/4. International Labour Organization, Geneva.

Hanlon, Joseph (1996). "Strangling Mozambique: IMF 'stabilization' in the world's poorest country." *Multinational Monitor* (July/August).

International Monetary Fund (2001). "Republic of Mozambique: selected issues and statistical appendix." IMF Country Report 01/25 (January). Available on the Internet at www.imf.org/external/pubs/ft/scr/2001/cr0125.pdf.

_____ (2000). "Tanzania: statistical annex." IMF Staff Country Report 00/122 (29 September). Available on the Internet at www.imf.org/external/country/tza/index.htm.

Mozambique, Government of (2000). *Republic of Mozambique: Interim Poverty Reduction Strategy Paper, Incorporating the Action Plan for the Reduction of Absolute Poverty (PARPA).* Maputo, 16 February (available on the Internet at www.imf.org/external/country/moz/index.htm).

Mozambique News Agency (2000). "Price of cashew nuts collapses." *AIM Reports* (6 December).

Tanzania, Government of (2000). *The United Republic of Tanzania: Poverty Reduction Strategy Paper.* Dar es Salaam, 1 October (available on the Internet at www.imf.org/external/country/tza/index.htm).

_____ (2000a). *The United Republic of Tanzania: Interim Poverty Reduction Strategy Paper.* Dar es Salaam, 14 March (available on the Internet at www.imf.org/external/country/tza/index.htm).

United Nations, Office for the Coordination of Humanitarian Affairs (2000). "Mozambique: IMF eases economic reform pressure." United Nations Integrated Regional Information Networks report (6 December).

Wallengren, Maja (1997). "A production slump hits Tanzanian coffee." *African Business News* (March).

World Bank (1996). *Tanzania: The Challenge of Reform: Growth, Income and Welfare.* Washington, D.C.

Part Two:

DEVELOPING COUNTRIES IN THE INTERNATIONAL ECONOMY

5

What foreign direct investors
provide and what they seek

ANDRE VAN HEEMSTRA[1]

Unilever provides a case study of the benefits that can accompany foreign direct investment (FDI). Unilever is a fast-moving consumer goods company, dedicated to meeting the "everyday needs of people everywhere" with branded food and home and personal care products. The company currently employs around 250,000 people worldwide. Our products are sold in 150 countries and we have an annual turnover of around $44 billion.[2] Over the last seventy years, Unilever has invested considerable resources in markets all around the world. We have invested for the long-term in the productive capacity of the local economy, and in one country after another we have seen the benefits that result.

The first benefit is employment. Foreign direct investment not only creates jobs directly, it usually supports additional employment up and down the supply chain. For example, Unilever currently employs around 6,000 people in the four South-East Asian markets of Indonesia, Thailand, Viet Nam and the Philippines. Yet our businesses in those markets also directly or indirectly support the jobs of 45,000 more people who work for our distributors, contractors, factory service suppliers and so on. In other words, in those markets, for every person we employ directly, we indirectly support at least seven or eight additional jobs. These figures don't include all those people employed by

---

[1]   Director, Unilever, The Netherlands.

[2]   Data of 1999. In 2000, Unilever merged with Bestfoods. As a result, the company now employs nearly 300,000 people and has an annual turnover of over $52 billion.

raw material suppliers and service providers, such as advertising agencies, who do not work exclusively for Unilever.

The second benefit of FDI is training and development. International companies normally invest significant resources in the transfer of professional skills. At Unilever, this includes substantial investment in the professional development of local managers and employees. This sort of investment helps to develop the skills base of the local economy and is particularly important in countries where government investment in education and training is relatively low.

The third benefit of FDI is the ripple effect up and down the supply chain. As competition intensifies, large corporations are increasingly focusing on their core businesses and outsourcing non-core functions and activities. This creates considerable opportunities for small and medium-sized enterprises. With companies also striving to make their supply chain networks as efficient as possible, business partners benefit from the technology inputs these systems require. This, combined with the need to meet international quality and service standards, helps to make local suppliers more competitive and strengthens both their market position and the local economy.

Critics sometimes claim that multinational companies reduce opportunities for local companies. However in our experience, for all the reasons outlined above, direct investment usually helps to fuel a "virtuous circle" of economic activity which, far from diminishing opportunities for local companies, actually creates more room for them to expand and grow.

Foreign direct investment is also a relatively stable source of investment–a point reinforced during the Asian economic crisis at the end of the 1990s. While short-term capital flows were dramatically affected, foreign direct investment remained high, and in some markets even increased. Direct investors took a responsible and long-term view—and they were encouraged to do so by the efforts that national governments had made to make their countries more attractive places to invest.

1. Deciding where to invest

When it comes to investment decisions, investors have to take into account a range of factors. They also have a great deal of choice. Over the last decade, viable investment options have expanded considerably, following the opening up of Central and Eastern Europe and China, and economic changes in Latin America, South-East Asia, Southern Africa and the Middle East. Not surprisingly, the competition for investment is fierce.

Investors are ultimately searching for market opportunities with good prospects for growth and attractive returns. They look for a political framework that is conducive to doing business and in which it is possible to operate according to global standards of corporate behaviour. They look for a level playing field in which rules, regulations and ways of doing business will not put them at a competitive disadvantage. They are looking for open, regionally integrated markets that offer economies of scale, an efficient infrastructure and a strong skills base.

Balancing risk and return

Investors are, fundamentally, looking for a good return on their investment. Company executives have a responsibility to their shareholders to make the best possible use of their capital, and they are accountable to these shareholders for their performance.

What constitutes a good balance of risk and return for any given company depends upon the nature of its business and its business strategy. In Unilever's case, we are dedicated to "meeting the everyday needs of people everywhere". We want to invest where we have access to markets or can grow with large numbers of consumers with "everyday needs" to be met.

In the next 25 years, 95 per cent of the world's population growth will be in what are now considered developing and emerging regions. Those same regions will account for 70 per cent of the increase in consumption. Given the nature of our business, these are clearly important markets for Unilever, and our investments in developing countries are long-term commitments.

Perceptions of whether a given market represents a good investment opportunity are also inevitably affected by perceptions of the political and economic context in which companies have to operate.

The key challenge for national governments is to make their countries as attractive as possible as places to invest. That requires action on both a political and economic level.

Good governance, political stability and the rule of law

Good governance and political stability are essential preconditions for attracting and retaining long-term investment. Good governance and stability give people confidence. Confident citizens make confident consumers. Investors seek out confident consumers so that they can invest to meet their growing needs.

Instability, in contrast, is bad for business and inhibits investment. Investors want to plan ahead with assurance and confidence, and they want to know that their property, people and investments are secure. Conflict, crime and political unrest undermine the confidence of consumers, employees and investors alike.

Investors also need to be sure that they can operate in a market unimpeded by corruption. They need to know that the only reason for a competitor's success is because it has a better product. They expect to be able to do business on a level playing field, and to operate according to clear standards and principles.

They are looking for transparency in legislation and administrative rules, and fairness in their implementation. They need to know that their businesses and local and expatriate employees will not be discriminated against, that their property rights will be respected and that all cases will be treated fairly. It is also essential for fundamental labour rights to be respected and applied.

The economic framework

International investors also seek to invest in stable economies, where macroeconomic conditions and government economic policies are conducive to doing business.

With companies considering investment options all around the world, a country has to ensure that its tax system, and employment and investment policies compare favourably with those elsewhere. Companies are also looking for a legal and regulatory framework that ensures effective competition.

Over the last five years, the economic framework has improved in most developing markets.

First, most countries have continued to make progress on reducing tariffs, import/export requirements and other barriers to trade. Simplifications to tariff systems have also helped to speed up the whole import-export process.

Second, many countries have reduced restrictions on ownership. Sectors of the economy previously considered strategic, such as power generation and telecommunications, have been opened up to private investment, and both consumers and business are enjoying more efficient services as a result.

Third, protections for intellectual property rights (IPR) have become more effective. Governments have a greater understanding of the importance of this, not only for international investors, but also for their own domestic businesses—particularly companies keen to expand internationally.

Fourth, governments of developing countries have made progress in reforming their domestic financial infrastructure, including appropriate supervision, opening up their financial services sectors to greater competition and doing more to integrate their financial services into global financial markets.

Finally, governments have a better understanding of the need to broaden the tax base. In some countries, a lot of work has been done in this area, including the introduction of sales taxes and initiatives to tackle tax evasion.

While the progress in these areas has been good, barriers to investment still remain. The process of liberalization and modernization still has further to go, and some countries are inevitably further behind than others. There are still problems with IPR protections, with over-complicated tax systems, and with restrictions on trade, ownership and foreign-currency transactions.

Nonetheless, it has been amply demonstrated that countries that liberalize their trade and investment regimes, thereby opening themselves up to the world economy, usually achieve higher rates of economic growth than those that have not done so.

This broader economic framework is also important to investors. They are looking for large, open, regional markets, in which it is possible to achieve effective economies of scale. This is a problem for those regions of the world, such as sub-Saharan Africa or Central America, where progress towards regional economic integration is less advanced than elsewhere. Regional institutions such as Mercosur in Latin America and ASEAN in South-East Asia are providing an important framework for progress towards reducing tariffs and removing barriers to cross-border trade and investment.

International investors are also seeking to invest in markets with a strong skills base, efficient transport and communication infrastructures and reliable supplies of energy, clean water and other basic services. Again, some developing and emerging markets have made considerable progress in these areas, and this puts less developed economies at a big disadvantage.

Doing business in a responsible and sustainable way

The final point to make is that multinational corporations expect to operate according to clear standards of corporate behaviour wherever they operate in the world. They know that in today's "global village", the way they operate everywhere has to be defensible to their shareholders, business partners and consumers anywhere.

There has been a belief in some quarters that by seeking to make their operations as efficient as possible, multinational companies drive down social and environmental standards, when in fact the opposite is more usually the case.

Far from seeing robust environmental protection and labour standards as a threat, multinationals welcome these standards, as long as they are fairly enforced. That is because they have their own global policies on environmental and employment issues, and they are unwilling to invest in markets in which weak regulation and enforcement allows others to gain a competitive advantage by operating to standards that they would regard as unacceptable and indefensible.

Developing world governments should not feel that they have to compromise in these areas in order to attract investment, when in fact the opposite is true. After all, some of the most competitive countries in the world, notably in Scandinavia, also have some of the highest standards of environmental and social protection.

Multinational corporations also increasingly recognize that the opportunities that flow from international trade and investment bring with them responsibilities. Host countries expect a "fair deal" between providing opportunities for investment and seeing their countries share in the benefits.

Companies such as Unilever are strongly integrated into the societies in which they operate, and the contribution they make to wider society extends beyond the direct economic benefits of investment. For example, all around the world Unilever is working in partnership with others to address specific local needs, through programmes to raise levels of education, improve health care, enhance the environment or support local economic development.

Initiatives such as the United Nations Global Compact and the OECD Guidelines for Multinational Enterprises are also important. The former brings a wide range of players together to take forward the contribution of business to development, and the latter helps to create a broad framework for responsible, sustainable investment.

2. Conclusion

FDI has a vital role to play in economic development. By supporting direct and indirect employment, strengthening the local skills base, injecting technology up and down the supply chain, and stimulating further local economic activity, foreign direct investment can contribute to a virtuous circle of wealth creation and economic development. Furthermore, companies investing around the world increasingly recognize the importance of doing business in a responsible and sustainable way.

At the same time, however, we should also be clear what foreign direct investment cannot do. It cannot make up for deficiencies in government policy in areas such as education or health care, and it cannot, on its own, be expected to cure a country's economic problems.

Companies wishing to invest in any given market expect to find a political and economic framework in which it is possible to do business efficiently and effectively. They want to invest in markets where there is good governance and political stability. They expect a level playing field and fair treatment in their dealings with public authorities and before the law.

They are looking for markets where good progress has been made in removing impediments to efficient business operations, including tariff and non-tariff barriers to trade and investment, and restrictions on ownership and trading rights. They are also looking for markets that are open and regionally integrated, and where there is a strong skills base and the infrastructure needed for effective operation.

Above all, however, companies are looking for investment opportunities with strong growth potential and the prospect of a good rate of return. When the investment options are as great as they are today, the right political and economic framework is necessary, but it is not in itself sufficient to attract substantial increases in investment.

Ultimately, investment decisions are about balancing risk and reward. International investors have a wide choice over where to invest in today's global market. They will go where the balance of risk and return is best.

6

Gender in international trade
and investment policy

MARIAMA WILLIAMS[1]

Of the world's 6 billion people, 2.8 billion live on less then US$2 a day, and 1.2 billion on less than a US$1 a day (World Bank, 2000). Most of these people are women, who today constitute the backbone of the unpaid, and a growing pool of the paid workforce that is directly affected by trade liberalization and foreign direct investment, as in export processing zones, agri-business and services. Women are also over-represented in the informal economy, sex tourism/trafficking, poverty and destitution. Women are the major cushion for domestic structural adjustment, as has been well documented in numerous case studies of structural adjustment programmes (see, for example, Afshar and Dennis, 1992; Brown, 1995; and Sparr, 1995).

Thus, there are important reasons for integrating a gender perspective into the themes of financing for development, especially foreign direct investment, other private capital flows and trade. We see these as inextricably intertwined with the topics of debt and systemic reform.

1. Trade and gender

The general aim of the multilateral trading system is trade expansion and trade intensification, with emphasis in liberalization negotiations on reciprocal exchanges of concessions, less attention to "special and differential treatment" and the erosion of preferences of developing countries. In such an

---

[1] International Gender and Trade Network; the Centre of Concern; DAWN, and DAWN-Caribbean.

environment the comparative advantage of developing countries seems to lie in cheap labour; increasingly, that cheap labour is female labour. Yet it is assumed either that trade liberalization will have the same effect on men and women, or that it is entirely beneficial to women.

In contrast, we believe that the potential gender impact of prospective changes in international trade policy needs to be explicitly assessed. The operations and governance of the multilateral and also regional trading system can have significant gender dimensions, and it is important to avoid false premises and misdiagnoses owing to lack of attention to such social relationships as gender. It is also relevant to ask gender-related questions about who decides and who is consulted in the decision-making process regarding trade provisions in the World Trade Organization (WTO) as well as provisions at the regional level. A further gender dimension focuses on the interplay between gender inequalities and gender biases on the one hand, and trade policies designed to facilitate export promotion and trade liberalization on the other hand.

The point is a little subtle. Gender does not play a significant role in the formulation of national trade negotiating positions and trade policy per se. However, gender bias in social and employment relations and gender inequalities in ownership, control and access to economic resources such as land, credit, and technical assistance play an important role in the multilateral trading system, to the detriment of women (UNCTAD, 1999). At the same time, trade expansion and trade intensification, as promoted by structural adjustment and other programmes of the World Bank and the International Monetary Fund, and the trade liberalization agenda of the WTO, presume the incorporation of women's labour in both the formal and informal sectors of the economy. In addition, the costs of adjusting to the consequences of trade liberalization (such as cuts in public services due to budget shortfalls from the reduction of trade tariffs) are disproportionately borne by women. Overall, liberalization and the economic adjustment it engenders or which accompanies it often lead to the intensification of women's caregiving activities (UNDP, 1995 and 1999).

2. International investment and gender

As in the case of trade liberalization, capital inflow is often held to be unambiguously good for the receiving economy. It is generally argued that private financial flows improve the quality of financial assets, engender competition, broaden and deepen the local capital and money markets and thus present the world's savers with a wider array of options for earning income on their decision to postpone consumption and provide investors with greater access to finance. However, recent events in Brazil, Mexico, the Russian Federation and South-East Asia have given cause for rethinking this logic, raising questions about the real benefits of these kinds of capital flows, which are destabilizing and occur in starts and stops, and which may or may not lead to growth but rather may lag behind it. Apart from these questions and the issue of the development dimension of financial flows, there are concerns about their gender impact.

Though there has been much research on export processing zones, there has been little examination of the gender impact of foreign direct investment (FDI) and other private capital flows in general. However, Braunstein (2000) attempted to capture the facts surrounding FDI and gender. She argued that, as with other macrolevel phenomena, the relation between FDI and gender operates at the macro-, "meso-" and microlevels. At the macrolevel, the feminization of the labour force impacts aggregate investment and savings patterns and the size and intensity of women's labour in the formal and informal sectors of the economy. At the mesolevel, there are issues of transaction costs, imperfect information, gender biases, market interlinkages, property rights and gender segmentation of markets. At the microlevel, the focus is usually on the division of responsibility between men and women, labour and power within households, gender-differentiated patterns of demand, differing patterns of control over assets, and the bargaining power and position outside the household for women and men.

Asking questions about possible linkages between gender and private capital inflows leads to other questions. For example, some women gain from FDI through their employment in export processing zones or multinational corporations, in general, and they seem to have increased educational opportunities associated with employment in areas dominated by multinational corporations in the export sectors. However, gaps between wage rates appear to persist. Other important questions that should be of concern to policy makers concerned with the development objectives of trade policy relate to the impact of heavy reliance on low-cost female labour on the competitiveness of the economy in the long run (are there limits to increasing female wages in the context of FDI?), and to the ability of FDI to promote gender equality in the long run.

3. Trade, finance and human rights

In this context, attention must also be paid to the role of the World Trade Organization, the International Monetary Fund and the World Bank as the key institutions promoting trade liberalization, and capital and investment liberalization. Many developing countries have adopted the programmes and follow the rules of the international financial institutions (IFIs) with the expectation of obtaining capital inflow. Whether or not the expected results materialize, there are also serious questions about constancy of the policies and broader considerations. This requires a comprehensive assessment of the trade and financial system and its connection with certain basic values, primary of which is the Universal Declaration of Human Rights, as well as other rights agreements, such as the Convention on the Elimination of All Forms of Discrimination against Women (CEDAW), the Declaration on the Right to Development and the Convention on the Rights of the Child.

In other words, we need an integrated framework for sustainable, gender-sensitive human development. In particular, trade policy should be seen as only one of many instruments (along with industrial policy, fiscal and monetary policies, etc.) that should aim at promoting gender equality, sustainable economic development, poverty eradication and the improvement in the standard of living of all citizens. Trade rules should be constrained and bound by international agreements that promote human rights, including women's rights, gender equality outcomes, ecological sustainability, human dignity and life. There should be fairness, transparency, democracy and participation by civil society in the international trading system, in particular, in WTO processes, including rule-making, negotiations, monitoring and dispute settlement.

4. Proposals

We therefore recommend a series of overall and sector-specific actions:

Overall considerations

- The Economic and Social Council of the United Nations should commission a comprehensive social and gender-sensitive review of the current processes of trade liberalization, trade expansion and trade intensification and their utility and efficacy for development, paying particular attention to the concerns of the poor and women.
- An independent focal point should be established to monitor the coherence and consistency between the policies and practices of WTO, IMF and the World Bank with regard to the programmes and operations of specialized UN agencies such as the Food and Agricultural Organization of the United Nations, World Food Programme and World Health Organization. It should also work to ensure that the emerging cross-conditionalities between the IFIs and the WTO system do not ex-

pand the power of international trade institutions beyond internationally agreed instruments and conventions such as the Universal Declaration of Human rights and CEDAW.

- The General Assembly of the United Nations should establish a commission to examine the implications of incorporating agricultural trade (in terms of food security) and intellectual property rights (in terms of access to biological resources and technology) under the umbrella of the WTO.

The reasons for a focus on these specific areas may be appreciated from the following more detailed proposals.

Food security

- Food security should be seen as a right, and measures to secure this right should be internationally guaranteed. Food aid cannot be a substitute for food self-sufficiency.
- International trade agreements on agriculture should take into consideration the particular situation of women farmers in the South, many of whom do not participate in commercial ventures but engage in farming for food self-sufficiency as a family activity passed down from generation to generation. Large-scale international commercial farmers pose a threat to traditional smallholders and to rural livelihoods as such.
- Women farmers and smallholders should be protected from unemployment, poverty and food insecurity. A clear distinction between the production of staple food crops for domestic consumption and the production of other crops for export should be drawn.
- Countries should plan and budget for food, just as they do for national security.

Intellectual property

- The international community should pass a resolution against the mandatory patenting of some life forms and some natural processes. Plants, animal and microorganisms should not be patentable. Furthermore, trade rules governing intellectual property rights must be in conformity with the Convention on Biological Diversity. Farmers must have the right to save and exchange seeds, as well as sell their harvest.
- The international community should guarantee access to essential medicines, including imports, especially for HIV/AIDs, and for other diseases that are impairing the lives of poor women and men.

- Traditional knowledge and the rights of local and indigenous communities over biological resources should be protected.
- An international commission should be established to examine the issue of the transfer of existing and new technology and the ways in which such transfers are constrained by the intellectual property rights regime of the multilateral trading system. Particular attention should be paid to the opportunities and challenges of technological development for women and marginal economic agents.

Workers at home and abroad

- Trade rules should be consistent with existing international agreements to promote human and women's rights, the environment and the dignity of life. They should be dedicated to the eradication of poverty.
- Corporations must be obligated to protect the human rights of male and female workers. In addition, there must be a mandatory and enforceable code of conduct for transnational corporations. This can be accomplish through a process of streamlining and strengthening the numerous existing codes of conduct under the auspices of a specially created entity or a specialized agency such as the United Nations Industrial Development Organization (UNIDO).
- Existing institutional mechanisms, particularly the International Labour Organization, must be strengthened to better protect labour rights, including greater attention to gender-specific worker rights issues, such as freedom from sexual harassment and sexual discrimination, access to day-care centres, menstruation leave and breastfeeding times.
- Trade rules should allow fewer impediments to the natural movement of persons. Movement of labour should be given at least the same special considerations as the movement of capital.
- Coordinated international efforts should be made to end international trafficking in women and girls.

International financial assistance

- The international community should guarantee the right of access to affordable essential services such as health care, education, water and energy.
- External debts should be cancelled in order to help reduce the budget constraints that many developing countries experience. This would

also help to liberate resources to help develop their domestic production capacity. This should be done in a gender-sensitive manner.

• An international fund should assist developing countries in strengthening supply capacity and meeting democratically agreed-upon trade commitments. Currently, the rules, the need to establish those rules, the technical assistance and the finance to implement such rules come from the international community. Countries need to develop an independent capacity for assessing the technical requirements of their economies and the best way to make changes, such that they promote poverty eradication and gender equality outcomes.

Domestic policy autonomy

• Governments should be allowed to maintain strategic policies on investment; finance and trade, including domestic content requirements; the promotion of universal service provision; and special programmes for vulnerable groups, especially women.

• Governments should encourage development of local firms and entrepreneurs through measures such as preferences and tax breaks to local investors, farmers and women entrepreneurs.

• Governments should retain the right to institute requirements on foreign investment in order to protect the balance of payments and meet the foreign exchange needs of the economy. These requirements include resorting to local content requirements, import restrictions, conditions on profit repatriation and retained earnings, and listing on a local stock exchange.

References

Afshar H., and C. Dennis, eds. (1992). *Women and Adjustment Policies in the Third World*. London: Macmillan.

Braunstein, E. (2000). Engendering foreign direct investment: household structures, labour markets and the international mobility of capital. *World Development,* Special Issue, vol. 28, No. 7 (July).

Brown, L. (1995). Gender and the implementation of structural adjustment in Africa: examining the micro-meso-macro linkages, a synthesis of a three country case study: Ghana, Zambia, Mali Report. Ottawa: Canadian International Development Agency; and Washington, D.C.: International Food Policy Research Institute.

Sparr, P. (1995). *Mortgaging Women's Lives: Feminist Critiques of Structural Adjustment,* 2nd edition. London: Zed Books.

UNCTAD (1999). *Trade, Sustainable Development and Gender.* New York and Geneva: United Nations Conference on Trade and Development.

United Nations Development Programme (1995). *Human Development Report 1995*. New York: Oxford University Press.

_____ (1999). *Human Development Report 1999*. New York: Oxford University Press for the United Nations Development Programme.

World Bank (2000). *World Development Report, 2000*. New York: Oxford University Press.

7

The global financial market
is vast and can be tapped

MARSHALL N. CARTER[1]

Current trends in demographics and world finance could have a powerful impact on the future of investing in emerging markets. State Street Corporation has an interesting perspective on these issues.

Having evolved over the past 25 years from a regional commercial bank into a global financial services company, State Street now handles staggering volumes of complex transactions that combine information technology with banking, securities processing, investment management and trade execution. State Street manages more than $700 billion in customers' assets and holds over $6 trillion in its custody, touching roughly 12 per cent of the over $50 trillion total world market for stocks, bonds and securities of all kinds every day.

State Street's role as custodian involves settling trades, safekeeping securities, keeping records, and a host of valuable services, including accounting across currencies; rapid, detailed data reporting; risk management and exposure reporting; real-time monitoring and analysis of investment performance; and many others. These activities generate billions of dollars in daily cash and transaction data flows and give custodians a bird's-eye-view of movements and trends within the world financial markets.

This experience in one company has implications for investment in developing nations. It involves the shift to global capital market finance and the ways in which developing economies can access the markets; the movement from geopolitics to geo-economics; the rate of technological development; and the Internet.

---

[1] Chairman, State Street Corporation, Boston.

These trends can be powerful forces for global peace and prosperity, but they present challenges too. How can emerging markets capitalize on these trends? What needs to be done?

What is it that investors are seeking when they consider investing in emerging markets?

1.   The shift to global capital market-based finance

For much of the last half of the 20th century, global capital markets have been displacing traditional banking as the key intermediators between providers and borrowers of capital.

Where this process of disintermediation is most advanced, as in the United States of America, roughly a third of all corporate finance now comes from banks. Capitalization of the United States stock market now exceeds 150 per cent of gross domestic product (GDP). Both the equity and debt markets in the United States are still growing, fueled by retirement savings from pensions, individual retirement accounts and 401(k)s, which are tax-advantaged savings vehicles, and other sources.

Total global equity market capitalization is estimated at over $31 trillion, just topping global GDP at $30 trillion, as estimated by the International Monetary Fund. However, over 40 per cent of this total global equity market capitalization is in the United States; less than 20 per cent is in continental Europe; and less than 10 per cent is in emerging economies. So, there is clearly enormous room for further growth of the world's stock and bond markets, particularly outside North America.

The major advantage of capital markets as a financing mechanism is that, together with the derivative markets for options and futures, these markets can "split the atom" of risk, hedge those risks and distribute that risk widely. Nations around the world are learning that they must act soon to spur the growth of capital markets that can, in turn, finance new economy industries. Nevertheless, countries that want to have access to capital markets also have the obligation to protect the investor.

When we look back just a few years prior to the crisis of 1997/98, we see that investors were attracted to emerging markets by a combination of impressive rates of economic growth and government incentives. The world has changed. Institutional investors today decide whether to invest in emerging markets based on a number of factors, not just promised rates of return.

To be players in the new global economy, developing nations need to take actions to provide confidence to investors and the markets, including:

- increased financial disclosure under internationally recognized accounting standards;

- a globally acceptable legal framework;
- improved debt management practices;
- coherent bankruptcy codes and financial market supervision;
- more market-based, less relationship-oriented banking systems;
- sound macroeconomic polices;
- sustainable currency exchange regimes.

Once such reforms are in place, emerging markets can mobilize domestic savings and attract far more in both direct investment and portfolio flows than they have ever received in foreign aid.

The key to success for emerging markets is the creation of a level playing field, which is only possible when, first, there is freedom from government interference; and second, there is complete transparency. Transparency means that the books and records, ownership, revenue streams, expenses, and everything related to the financial performance and ownership of companies are open and clear for all to see.

2. Moving from geopolitics to geo-economics

We are now witnessing a hopeful movement, in much of the world, away from military competition and warfare towards a common quest for prosperity and growth.

While there is obvious concern about some regions, this move away from warfare to economic competition is a growing trend. Total world military expenditures have declined by one third since 1989. From 1992 to 1998, armed conflicts declined in all the world's five major regions, from 55 to 36.

The movement towards "geo-economics" is being driven by many factors. World capital markets have been growing steadily and have become more integrated. World trade has been outpacing the growth of domestic economies for decades. National borders are becoming less relevant as regulation is liberalized and tariff and non-tariff barriers disappear. In addition, technology has enabled us to leverage knowledge and talent worldwide.

In the United States alone, net international investment has grown from 3 per cent of GDP in 1990 to 14 per cent of GDP in 1998.

Institutional investors such as pension funds are leading the trend to cross-border investment. In 1990, for example, non-home country investment by pension funds worldwide was less than US$350 billion dollars. It is expected to top US$3 trillion dollars in the next few years. Cross-border capital flows to emerging nations already dwarf all official foreign aid by a factor of roughly six to one, US$240 billion a year versus US$40 billion.

Part of this shift is due to declining official foreign aid, and, in large part, to "donor fatigue." However, the bulk of new private capital flows to developing economies simply come from the vast new pools of capital available today. Total global pension, collective fund and insurance capital grew from US$10 trillion in 1990 to US$36.5 trillion last year, and are projected to total over US$60 trillion by 2004. Furthermore, the managers of these funds, for risk management and asset diversification purposes, are continually creating a broad spectrum of innovative investment choices, tools and strategies.

Technology and the Internet

The Internet's future growth prospects are enormous in the developing world. It can also help developing countries take advantage of the major trends in global finance.

The World Wide Web will force a more profound restructuring of capital markets in the next few years than the financial world has seen over the past two centuries. It will link stock and bond markets nationally, perhaps even globally; it will dramatically lower trading costs; and it will level the playing field by providing a wealth of information and analytical tools to ordinary people as well as to institutional investors.

The Internet and other new communications technologies offer tremendous potential benefits to the developing world but there are challenges too. Today over half of the North American population has access to the Web at home or at the office. In the developing world, that ratio is only one out of every hundred.

The politics of globalization

Trade and investment can be "win-win" transactions for national economies, but many legitimate concerns about the impacts of globalization must be addressed to ensure a positive outcome.

In developed nations, the global economy is often viewed with suspicion, as evidenced by the public demonstrations around recent trade meetings in the United States. To resolve these concerns, we need to understand and deal with a host of issues including the employment of displaced workers, protection of labour rights, the environment and the economic impacts of cross-border investment flows.

In emerging markets, there is plenty of room for positive growth and access to these tremendous new pools of capital. However, these markets need first to develop the legal, financial and technological infrastructure to reap those benefits.

Finally, in order to create a global economy that benefits us all, we need strong, courageous political leadership around the world.

8

Why is there not more international project financing for emerging economies today?

TOM MARSHELLA[1]

One thing remains clear when looking at the current state of infrastructure financing in emerging markets: demand for capital investment continues to far outstrip supply. Current estimates of the demand for global infrastructure financing over the next 10 years run the gamut from US$1 to US$2 trillion. Individual estimates are so large and diverse that any discussion of their accuracy is likely to prove pointless. But even using the most conservative among these estimates, one can easily see the imbalance in the current supply and demand equation.

On the supply side, figures are more certain. Privately arranged domestic and cross-border investment—including rated bank loans, Rule 144A private placements and direct foreign lending—totals only US$71 billion for projects worldwide for the last nine years combined. This leaves a tremendous shortfall to be funded in the public markets which, for a variety of reasons that we will explore later, have fluctuated over the past several years between a cold and a lukewarm reception to such investments.

One of the reasons that projects from developing countries continue to experience difficulties in accessing the public debt markets is that the assessment of the risks involved in such investments is still an embryonic discipline. Since such financings were historically funded privately, there is not a lot of public data available on the performance of such investments, either on a stand-alone basis or as an asset class. This lack of performance data has made it

[1] Managing Director, Moody's Investors Service, New York.

very difficult for investors to get comfortable with these investments initially. Then, once involved, a continued lack of information has also made these investments very difficult to monitor. Even as public debt financing becomes more common, it has been difficult to build a track record for projects as an asset class as a whole. Few projects are alike in either purpose or structure, which makes it very difficult to extrapolate the performance of or lessons learned from one and apply them to another.

The assignment of public debt ratings to individual projects has improved the flow of information and introduced an element of comparability across projects and between projects and other types of investments, but the rating of projects is likewise a relatively young discipline. Moody's assigned the first public debt rating to a project in 1991, and rated the first cross-border, non-U.S. transaction in 1994. Today, we maintain ratings on over 240 bonds and loans in nearly 30 countries.

Still, no one really knows how these projects will behave as an asset class during an extreme and prolonged crisis of confidence, other, of course, than the lessons that we have learned from Asia. The story there has not been promising.

1. Vulnerability in the face of legal, regulatory and political risk

In the mid-1990s, Moody's was among the presenters at conferences with optimistic titles such as "Preparing for the Asian infrastructure boom " and "Funding Asian infrastructure: '94, '95, '96". Today, instead of an Asian boom, our deal queue has slowed to a trickle, and we are asked to speak at conferences with titles such as "Restructuring your Asian projects" and "Limiting your downside in project renegotiation."

This is not to say that some Asian countries have not done outstanding jobs financing their infrastructure needs. However, the recent experiences of capital-market lenders to regional projects has not been typified by euphoria. Indeed, much money has been lost. Nearly 70 per cent of Asian project debt rated during the mid-1990s has either been downgraded or had its outlook revised downward by Moody's. Exactly half of these have defaulted, and of those that have not, only one is considered investment grade.

The primary cause of the defaults and downgrades was, as everywhere, economic. However, what differentiated Asian projects was the way in which the structures set up to mitigate these economic risks unravelled almost as soon as they were put to the test. Counterparts who had accepted risk repudiated that risk when it occurred. Legal systems simply proved unable to enforce the contracts as agreed. Regulatory approvals that had been held out as straightforward proved anything but when projects moved to the operations stage. And, above all, the political will that had been so apparent in getting the projects financed evaporated when the projects needed support in a time of crisis.

Examples abound. In Indonesia, the credibility of dollar-linked electricity tariffs as mitigants of currency exposure was destroyed as PT PLN Persero (PLN) and the government refused to honor such tariffs when faced with massive devaluation. In China, an experiment with the use of municipal "rate covenant" structures—so prevalent in financing infrastructure in the United States—failed ignominiously with the default of Zhu Hai Highway Company, Limited. Regulators simply proved unable or unwilling to raise toll rates to increase revenues in the way that had previously been agreed. Elsewhere in China, Panda Global Energy also needed restructuring as it found it impossible to implement a previously agreed tariff for its power supplies.

We believe, based on these and other experiences, that many of the issues keeping investors at bay go beyond the structuring of individual deals to the systemic risks involved in emerging market economies as a whole. The difficulties faced by many Asian projects clearly demonstrate that—regardless of financial structuring—the ultimate determinant of credit worth for a project is its underlying economics, which can change dramatically as the result of external shocks that are difficult to either predict or hedge against. They also clearly indicate that, regardless of how the contracts are structured, these contracts are worth little more than the paper on which they are written if the legal and political system of the host country cannot guarantee that they will be consistently enforced. We believe that the skids of liquidity will not be greased for project financing in these countries until some of these larger issues are specifically addressed.

2. Investment shifts to more mature economies, new deal structures

Since the Asian crisis, project and infrastructure investors have flocked to more developed economies. In an effort to "right size" their federal, state, or local government budgets, as well as introduce competition for basic services, they have attracted private debt capital inflows via asset sales and restructuring monopoly businesses. Clearly, investors who have moved to these markets perceive a more palatable risk/reward mix outside of emerging economies. The flight to quality has been motivated in part by the presence of mature legal systems, the relatively strong credit quality of project off-takers,[2] and the willingness of investors to lend material sums in domestic currency, that is, the

---

[2] For example, electricity distribution companies that would purchase the output from a power plant. — Eds.

same currency in which project cash flows are denominated. Examples of such recent, successful deals outside of Asia include Integrated Accommodation Services, a 400 million pounds sterling (£) office automation private finance initiative (PFI) transaction wrapped by a monoline insurer[3] and rated Aaa, and AES Drax, a £650 million coal-fired power plant, which has Baa3 and Ba2 rated tranches.

However, even developed economies have been able to attract less infrastructure capital than they would like. Regardless of domicile, projects nearly always take longer than originally envisioned to reach financial close. Indeed, most projects have the gestation period of an elephant, or worse. This trend helps explain why some of the most promising project venues continue to experience funding shortfalls, even when capital markets are awash with liquidity and capital availability.

One factor that has helped to increase investor receptivity to some deals has been the innovative manner in which their financing has been structured. While project finance has traditionally combined aspects of fundamental and "structured" finance, it is clear that elements in the financial structuring of projects are playing a greater role in attracting lenders. The definition of a project gets more and more muddied as individual deals take on greater and greater levels of financial engineering and structuring, with an eye towards providing higher degrees of flexibility and market liquidity.

As a case in point, project-focused hedge funds are presently looking for financial structures that would provide quick access to primary market capital for projects with certain predetermined risk profiles. Export credit notes[4] have played a role in attracting funds for new export lending in the last few years. Similarly, collateralized debt obligations (CDOs) have provided project underwriters and developers with a tool for liquefying loan portfolios, thereby freeing up capital for new asset level lending.[5]

Nevertheless, another very significant, but counter-development is that bonds and loans are being issued with common security agreements and only slightly different terms—in other words, there is more commonality in the financial structures of different types of credits. This has helped to increase

---

[3]   A monoline insurer is a third party that enters a financial transaction and assumes the credit risk. It is a type of financial guarantor. — Eds.

[4]   These are notes backing export credits and are a form of securitizing future flows. — Eds.

[5]   In other words, commercial banks can take loans that they have made, pool and structure them, and on-sell to the public. This tool is especially important for banks that have reached their limits in making loans to a particular sector. By wiping the slate clean, CDOs allow the banks to undertake further lending. — Eds.

issuer receptivity to certain financings because they can progress with the financing, knowing that if one market is closed to them (typically the bond market), then the bank market will still be there without large-scale restructuring of the transaction.

These developments—coupled with the holy trinity of privatization, corporatization and increasing market liberalization—have led to more deals being undertaken on a pure commercial basis and fewer fast track, "favoured-son" projects.

Finally, with more market and commodity risk has come increasingly diverse credit ratings. New ratings assigned over the past year have ranged from Aaa for monoline-insured projects located in the United Kingdom and Spain to Ba3 stand-alone projects in the United States. Each such project has attracted its own set of investors based on its ability to communicate effectively its own unique risks to analysts and investors, and to offer a return commensurate with those risks in the eyes of at least a few. Debt investors are keenly aware that credit risk is a zero-sum game. They are not necessarily adverse to risk; they do, however, want these risks identified.

3. Information must flow before capital will

The conventional wisdom has long offered reasons why new debt issuance volumes are relatively low for projects in emerging economies. These reasons include the following:

Domestic debt markets are not deep, and adequate lending capacity has not yet developed in these countries, which leaves local projects dependent almost solely on cross-border investors for funding;

Project counterparties do not have known track records and sometimes are of questionable credit standing, which limits their ability to attract investors;

- A lack of demographic data or an unwillingness on the part of project sponsors or local governments to aggregate or share data on existing and projected demand limits the ability of analysts and investors to judge accurately the economic feasibility of the project and potential demand risk;
- Projects are often too large for investor appetites. Investors have long sought to diversify their exposure to "story" paper [6]. Projects that are larger and involve rapid increases in expenditure can present significant concentration risk to project investors. Also, the sheer financial and potential operating magnitude of some projects could make them easy political targets. How would a government behave if, for example, severe construction

---

[6]   These are smaller and less well-known projects. — Eds.

problems were encountered, or demand was significantly misforecast?

- The development of a sound legal infrastructure has often not preceded the development of physical infrastructure. Simply put, creditors need a system that will act expediently to protect their rights. Project finance is typically a pyramid of contracts. In many countries, investors simply do not know whether these contracts will be upheld as legal, binding or enforceable, or whether they or other parties will be allowed to behave in accordance with the contracts' terms;

- Political and regulatory risks tend to be higher and are less able to be circumscribed in emerging market countries because of this same lack of legal infrastructure. In other words, the law cannot protect an investor from a government that simply changes its mind.

However, Moody's believes that there is also another reason that is often overlooked when explaining this funding shortfall: the financial and operational performance of many projects is very difficult to monitor. The disclosure of quarterly or annual financial performance and of the impact of "material events" is erratic or non-existent for most projects. This is a legacy of their historical private funding as well as of their undeveloped accounting rules and regulatory requirements. Combined with the fact—as noted above—that the legal and regulatory processes of most of these countries are likewise inconsistent and opaque, the costs of researching and monitoring these projects are simply too high for most investors to make it worth their while.

The role of public debt ratings has been a very important one in providing an independent third-party assessment of the credit risks involved in project financings and in providing ongoing monitoring of these projects' performance. Nevertheless, even for the rating agencies, such assessments are a laborious and time-intensive process that combines fundamental analysis, structured finance expertise, a heavy reliance on their sovereign risk units to help determine which way the political winds are blowing, and a healthy dose of investigative reporting. For Moody's to determine the real story behind any given project usually requires asking the same question hundreds of different ways to sponsors, government officials, regulators, managers, and operational personnel. Even then, for all the same reasons we have outlined above, we cannot be sure that we have the real story.

We believe that until such time as these issues are addressed, funding for emerging market projects in public debt markets will continue to fall short of those lofty projected capital demand numbers we noted earlier. However, we do believe that these obstacles will eventually be overcome. It will take commitment and some creativity, but we believe that capital can and will eventually flow to where it is needed for emerging economy infrastructure.

9

An investor's perspective on corporate governance in emerging markets

CHERYL HESSE[1]

Corporate governance has become a major discussion topic among investors who purchase corporate securities, especially securities of firms from emerging markets. This chapter seeks to explain why corporate governance has become so prominent recently. It concludes with a look at how one major investor, Capital International, Inc., perceives the corporate governance issue.

1. What is corporate governance and why is it important to emerging economies?

Corporate governance refers to the interlocking sets of laws, regulations, listing rules, corporate codes and judicial systems that govern the relationships among shareholders, directors and managers of corporations. Corporate governance codes or best practices guides have been adopted by many organizations, from stock exchanges, such as the Stock Exchange of Hong Kong; to supranational organizations, such as the Organisation for Economic Cooperation and Development (OECD); to institutional investors, such as the California Public Employees Retirement System. These codes identify the characteristics that adherents believe to be hallmarks of good corporate governance.

These characteristics tend to fall into a few categories: transparency, equitable treatment and accountability. The first category is transparency. Best

[1] Vice President and Senior Counsel, Capital International, Inc., Los Angeles. The opinions expressed in this chapter are those of the author and not necessarily those of Capital International, Inc. or its employees.

practices here include adherence to established accounting norms and annual audits that permit an investor to evaluate corporate performance. They would also include fair disclosure of ownership structure, voting rights and executive compensation, and disclosure regarding related party transactions.

The second set of issues deals with the equitable treatment of shareholders. Best practices here would include the concept of one share equals one vote, and equitable treatment of minority shareholders in takeover situations.

The third category concerns accountability. Best practices generally call for corporate boards of directors to have enforceable fiduciary duties to a corporation and its shareholders. They recommend processes for resolving potential conflicts of interest in favour of the corporation and its shareholders, over those of individual board members.

This focus on corporate governance has implications for emerging markets that are difficult to ignore. Over the next 20 years, emerging market economies are expected to experience significantly higher growth rates than developed economies. They are also expected to account for more than two thirds of overall global economic growth during that time. As an investor, the potential growth is compelling, but not determinative. One factor that investors will consider as they search for value in these markets is the degree to which the country and the company have adopted sound corporate governance practices. In fact, a recent McKinsey survey showed that investors from all over the globe would pay between 18 and 27 per cent premiums for companies with effective corporate governance *(McKinsey Investor Opinion Survey,* June 2000).

There is also plenty of evidence within markets that those companies that feature high standards of corporate governance have also achieved higher valuations than other companies in similar industries within the same country or region. That element alone lowers the cost of capital for these companies allowing for additional growth opportunities. Some examples of this would include, in Mexico, Wal Mart de Mexico, and more recently Telmex; and in Asia, Taiwan Semiconductor Technology Corporation and Infosys Technologies.

Proper corporate governance is also critical to capital market development over the long run. This is true for domestic as well as foreign investors. Many emerging economies have begun comprehensive pension schemes that invest in domestic fixed income securities and equities. The long-run success of these programmes is critical to the development of the economies and is a primary source of domestic capital accumulation. It is in the interest of all of us to have the infrastructure for good capital market development in place. Corporate governance is a keystone to that foundation.

The emphasis on corporate governance appears to be spreading. Western investors may have voiced some of the initial concerns, but the cause is now championed by diverse groups from around the world. Some examples include the Asian Corporate Governance Association; in Kenya, the Private Sector Initiative for Corporate Governance; and in the Republic of Korea, the Participatory Economic Committee of People's Solidarity for Participatory Democracy. Germany has created a stock market that limits listings to companies that adhere to certain principles of corporate governance, and Brazil is investigating doing the same. In addition, over 330 attendees from 25 countries attended a meeting of the International Corporate Governance Network held in New York in July of 2000.

2.   Why is this examination occurring now?

A number of factors are contributing to the current emphasis on corporate governance, including the increase in privatization and the 1997 Asian financial crisis that spread to other emerging markets.

During the past decade, the governments of many emerging market economies have broadened the base of investment in their countries by privatizing companies previously run by the State. While private investors entered, State agencies sometimes continued to hold controlling stakes in the corporations and to wield influence and pressure on the corporations as if the outside investors were not present. In many instances, the liberalization of financial systems seems to have outpaced the development of sound corporate governance practices.

The financial crisis that began in Asia in 1997 highlighted the risks of investing in countries with poor corporate governance. Individual companies failed, in part owing to weak capital market regulation and a failure to protect minority shareholders. These individual failures created uncertainty in the minds of investors that quickly undermined confidence in the countries as a whole. Indeed, concerns with corporate governance seem to have contributed to the spread of the Asian financial crisis to Latin America and the Russian Federation.

As developing nations increasingly permit and encourage the use of private sources of capital, incidents such as those noted above temper investors' enthusiasm for investing in those nations. However, the incidents are also bringing together such parties as international investors and local governments for discussion of how to work to effect change.

International investors have cooperated with the governments of developing nations to encourage reform. For example, in 1997 a Chilean public utility negotiated a deal to sell the company without calling a board meeting.

The deal provided certain inside shareholders with 300 times the value given to other minority shareholders. In the wake of that corporate governance failure, many international investors provided an investor perspective to local parties negotiating new tender-offer legislation. Again that year in Argentina, local law permitted a controlling shareholder to acquire a local corporation and delist its shares without requiring shareholder approval for the delisting. Shareholders prohibited from owning illiquid shares were forced to participate in the tender offer at a price that some long-term shareholders believed to be inadequate. Again, international investors worked with local parties to help implement legislation narrowing the risk of similar future transactions.

A current example of this type of cooperation is the work of the Brazilian Securities Commission (CVM), which recently hosted a group of major institutional emerging market investors at a meeting with representatives of many of the largest public corporations in Brazil. Legislation implementing a number of sound corporate governance measures is currently pending in the Brazilian legislature and is supported by the Central Bank and the Ministry of Finance. The meeting was designed to permit a dialogue between corporations and investors regarding the potential benefits to those corporations of such legislation.

Although the emphasis on corporate governance has increased in recent years, the important message is that this emphasis is not a fad. This effort is an integral part of the globalization of world markets that both investors and developing countries will need to address.

3. The perspective of a major investor

Capital International, Inc., is one of the largest investors in emerging markets, investing over US$25 billion on behalf of its institutional clients. It is a "bottom-up", research-oriented investor. Last year, its 31 dedicated emerging markets analysts made over 1,700 company visits to obtain information relevant to deciding where to invest its managed assets. In my role as Vice President and Senior Counsel of Capital International, I chair its internal corporate governance working group.

A *Wall Street Journal* article published in early November 2000 was entitled, "Corporate governance issues hamper emerging markets–stalled changes push some shareholders to abandon the field". Capital International, Inc., has not by any means been pushed to abandon the field. However, our firm has been challenged by our clients to demonstrate how we will deal with the challenge of corporate governance in emerging markets.

We are, as I mentioned, a bottom-up, research-driven investor. We tend to be long-term investors, focusing on portfolio companies that we expect to hold for at least several years. Our analysts and portfolio managers actively investigate factors relevant to decisions to become and remain shareholders. Corporate governance has always been a factor in choosing portfolio investments. Capital International has developed an internal version of corporate governance best practices, which our analysts refer to when investigating a potential investment.

Several recent incidents have propelled our company to become more involved in highlighting the need for corporate governance reform. We are engaged in this role in three ways. First, and most importantly, our analysts use their company visits and discussions with corporate decision makers to discuss corporate governance concerns and recommend improvements. Second, when such individual efforts fail, Capital International has voiced concerns with regulatory agencies and legislatures in emerging markets to support broad-based reforms. On the domestic side we have met with investment banks that sponsor American Depositary Receipts (ADRs).[2] We have encouraged them to support Depositary Agreements that protect an ADR investor's ability to vote proxies of ADR companies and to receive rights to distributions similar to those of local investors. In limited circumstances, we have carefully considered and have engaged in litigation designed to correct illegal corporate governance practices. Third, we participate in several multilateral organizations whose goals include educating governments and corporations about the benefits of responsible corporate governance, and helping to implement beneficial changes. One of these is the Global Corporate Governance Forum that is a joint effort of the World Bank and the OECD.

Capital International recognizes the need for continued and expanded dialogue on the issue of corporate governance—not only in emerging markets, but also in developed markets. We also recognize that there is no one set of principles that will work for all nations. Corporate governance reform must be undertaken within the context of local conditions, giving due regard to a country's corporate history and culture.

For Capital International, the conduct of corporate governance is of paramount importance, and we therefore require assurance that the companies in which we invest will run strictly on the basis of commercial considerations. Failure to adhere to the basic tenets of corporate governance may cause us to

---

[2]   Companies, often from emerging economies, can indirectly raise equity capital on the United States financial markets through ADRs. One attraction is that companies that cannot meet the strong corporate reporting requirements for a direct listings for example, on the New York Stock Exchange, may be able to satisfy the requirements for an ADR issue. — Eds.

lose confidence in investment opportunities offered by particular companies or countries.

We have been investing in emerging markets since 1979. As long-term investors, we know the benefits of understanding all relevant investor risks and of patience in realizing growth and change. While we remain committed to the process of improving corporate governance, we also will invest our clients' assets with due regard to the potential risks that corporate governance lapses bring.

Capital International is very pleased that the United Nations has targeted proper development of emerging markets as a priority in the years to come. We, of course, would like to offer our assistance to any effort that improves the environment for capital markets in developing countries.

Part Three:

EVOLVING NATIONAL FINANCIAL SYSTEMS AND POLICIES

10

Financing for development in the context of national development planning

ROBERTO RUBIO-FABIÁN[1]

On the subject of financing for development, as on the subject of the mobilization of domestic resources, there are at least three basic questions to consider:

- What is it that we want to finance? In which direction do we want to mobilize the resources that we have?
- How do we want to finance? How should we internally mobilize the resources?
- With whom do we want to finance? With whom should we carry out the domestic resource mobilization?

The first question leads us to what kind of strategy or development process we wish to finance or where we want to direct the funds. This means defining the aim of the development strategy to be financed, which confronts us with the problems of allocation and utilization of the funds (to what end are we allocating and utilizing the funds?).

The second question deals with the problems of raising and channelling financial resources in order to encourage the development process. That is, how and from where to obtain the funds? Through which structures and mechanisms should they be channelled? How should we mobilize our internal funds?

---

[1]   Executive Director, National Development Foundation of El Salvador (FUNDE), and Co-ordinator of the Structural Adjustment Participatory Review International Network (SAPRIN) for Latin America.

Here it is important to indicate that the process of mobilization of domestic resources, as with financing for development in general, cannot and should not be reduced to resolving the problem of obtaining funds. The national mobilization of funds should above all take into account the destination and use of these resources. For example, in order for internal savings to play an essential role in financing for development, it is not sufficient simply to make efforts to increase the rate of internal savings and elevate the amount of financial savings. It is also necessary to guarantee that the financial savings are converted into real savings, channelling the financial savings thus generated into investments. This is directly connected to guaranteeing the structural conditions, which open the door to investment opportunity and assure the quality and appropriate destination of the funds (e.g., investments consistent with development objectives; assuring adequate spatial distribution of the investments; promoting investments with high levels of added value, productivity and interconnection; channelling investments into accumulation processes towards small and medium-sized businesses; and ecosystem-friendly investments).

The third question refers to the social groups that intervene in the processes of domestic mobilization of funds and therefore confronts us with the problems of distribution and allocation of profits or resources. Who should participate in the process of mobilization of domestic funds? Which social groups make sacrifices for or benefit from this process?

With respect to the third question, it is important to consider that the processes of obtaining, allocating and utilizing profits occur within the framework of specific relationships and social structures. They are processes that pass through the power structures and vested interests that characterize different societies. From this point of view, it must not be forgotten that opting to finance development is not, and cannot be, detached from the conflicts generated by the social dispute over profits. Therefore, it is not possible to approach the question of mobilization of domestic resources adequately and realistically without taking into account, in each individual country or region, the characteristics of its organisms of power and self-interest, its existing structural inequalities and the nature and quality of its institutions. In this sense, a strategy or policy of domestic mobilization of funds should count on a power map and an "institutional map" that take into account the socio-institutional framework within which a strategy or policy concerning the domestic mobilization of funds is registered.

For example, a policy to mobilize domestic funds through the implementation of tax increases could result in resistance or evasion by powerful economic and political groups, and the pressure would be diverted to sectors that are more disadvantaged or have less capacity to negotiate. This would have the effect of forcing tax policy towards the raising of indirect taxes (more so than direct taxes) or broadening the taxable income range to include lower incomes.

Having explored the aforementioned ideas, the remainder of this chapter sets out to analyse how the first two questions have been answered as well as the attempts still being made to answer them through a concrete experience: the process of developing the National Plan *(Plan de Nación)* in El Salvador.

What proposal or development process can drive a strategy for the mobilization of domestic resources? The answer that some sectors in El Salvador gave was the elaboration and implementation of a National Plan. The early stages of this process date back to May of 1997. The project was carried out by the National Development Commission *(Comisión Nacional de Desarrollo–CND),* an independent, pluralistic commission appointed by the former President of El Salvador, Armando Calderon Sol. This initiative created a limited but significant national process of participation and civic mobilization, contributing to the presentation, in January 1998, of the first formal proposal, the Bases for the National Plan *(Bases para el Plan de Nación).* This document, which originated from and is founded on social dynamics, defined the theoretical, methodological and programming bases of the process and serves as a frame of reference for taking the process forward. Later, in October of 1999, in the context of a new Government presided over by President Francisco Flores, the CND, supported by continuous civic consultation, presented a second and more polished proposal to the three powers of the State: Initial Actions for the National Plan *(Plan Acciones Iniciales del Plan de Nación).* This proposal outlined broad strategic aims of national development and the general instruments needed for implementation. Subsequently, after almost a year of work, in October of 2000, the CND elaborated a third, concrete proposal to be agreed and put into action in the year 2001: the proposal for Territorial Actions for the National Plan (propuesta de *Acciones Territoriales del Plan de Nación).* This proposal details the aims and the specific, immediate steps to be taken within the development process of the National Plan.

The current proposal of the CND, as in its previous documents, is based on the fact that the most important challenge facing El Salvador is overcoming the structural marginalization and exclusion of large segments of the population. Therefore, the question that immediately arose was where to begin resolving this historical problem. According to the CND proposal, the best way to set national development in motion was to take a bottom-up approach which implied establishing and implementing development regions. This reflects CND support for regional development as a concrete measure leading to national development. Five large regions of development would be established and each one assigned a "horizon", or direction to guide its transformation. Thus, an agro-environmental corridor is planned for the North/Lempa region, the Gulf of Fonseca/Río Grande de San Miguel region is to be converted into a Central American gateway to worldwide commerce and an agricultural and agro-industrial development zone; the Central South/Comalapa region is to be converted into a sustainable export corridor, while the challenge facing the Western/Los Volcanos region is to develop an ecotourism and coffee corridor; finally, the proposal contemplated for the metropolitan area of San Salvador is the transformation of its system of roads.

Contrary to previous proposals, the CND proposal does not focus exclusively on the macro, but is based on revitalizing the micro. The proposal does not address "the national" level in general but gets down to the specific territories. Another difference is that it was not designed technocratically, without consultation; it is the product of a limited but significant participatory process. Unlike other proposals, it does not give unilateral support to external factors, but bases the external on the workings of our production systems at an internal, or national, level. Nor is it based on creating a "dam" to divert resources to only a chosen few, as was the case with previous proposals, but on the integration of those in society who have historically been excluded and marginalized. It is not the case of one glass overflowing, but of many glasses being filled.

Aside from looking for and crystallizing social and political consensus for the proposal for Territorial Actions, the CND seeks to respond to our second question: where to get the funds necessary to promote the proposal, and through what structures or mechanisms should they be channelled? The answers to these questions have still not been determined, but a process for defining them is taking shape. For the moment, only some elements relating to this matter can be examined.

Some sources for the mobilization of domestic resources can be identified on a provisional basis. Firstly, a prerequisite for the mobilization of resources is public income and expenses. In effect, taxation collects a large part of the profits and resources generated in a society, and these funds are reallocated and distributed through public spending. Consequently, the adequate mobilization of funds for development requires a fiscal policy that maintains high levels of taxation and an effective and efficient allocation of public spending. However, in the majority of the countries in the South we find, on the one hand, low levels of tax collection and, on the other hand, high levels of inefficiency, corruption and waste in public spending. For this reason, a prerequisite of any process of mobilization of domestic resources is fiscal reform.

Fiscal reform should contemplate, at minimum, the following components or policies:

- A change of objectives. The predominant fiscal policies are defined almost exclusively in terms of financing the fiscal deficit. Other objectives of fiscal reform should be to improve income distribution; to attract and reorient investments to match the objectives of the development strategy; and to be able to stimulate or contain demand or consumption and cover the programmed levels of public investment;
- The correction of the growing imbalance that favors establishing indirect taxes over direct taxes;
- The creation or increase of selective consumer taxes, particularly on those products that are harmful to public health or the environment;
- The creation of a "green" tax on activities that are harmful to the environment;
- The uniform establishment, in each country, of a tax on income earned through speculation or short-term investments;
- Measures to curb tax evasion;
- Administrative and financial reorganization of State-owned and private companies;
- Encouragement of a greater balance between ordinary public spending and public expenditure on investments;
- Improvement of the geographic distribution of public investment, currently mainly concentrated on a few cities, and a focus on infrastructure investment for the disadvantaged and excluded productive sectors.

Thus, the adequate mobilization of domestic funds requires financial reform, which should take into account three areas of action:

- The reform of the private system of financial mediation, allowing for a more modern and competitive market structure and putting an end to the oligopoly of the current financial system;
- A tightening of levels of supervision and control over the financial system (central bank and superintendencies);
- The creation of a financial system for development, which, by consolidating existing institutions (*Banco Multisectorial de Inversiones* [in El Salvador]), could become a real development bank specializing in supporting small and medium-sized businesses.

A basic variable in the process of mobilizing domestic resources is the structuring of internal savings. A basic point to consider in consolidating a process of structuring internal savings is the reform of the pension system. It is necessary to reform the existing pension system in order to create a mixed system based on solidarity (private enterprise, State and workers), which would permit a significant increase in the income and savings of the workers as well as an increase of income to the public finance sector.

Local compensation funds, or funds created through processes of local or territorial coordination, represents another important source of domestic financing.

In processes of mobilization of domestic resources, it is also important to consider the regulation and stimulation of investment. With regard to investment regulation, the effect of taxes on gross capital formation is important. In this sense, a system of fiscal incentives/inhibitors should be contemplated in order to stimulate/pressure the reinvestment of company profits.

Finally, reforms to the public administration and the General National Budget (*Presupuesto General de la Nación*) are necessary in order to reduce noticeably the excessive proportion of ordinary public spending over expenditure on investment.

According to the proposal for Initial Action and the proposal for Territorial Actions of the National Plan, these diverse sources of fund-raising should be channelled through two large funds: the territorial fund for development (*fondo territorial de desarrollo*) for business and production investment, and the community and municipal investment fund (*fondo de inversiones comunitarias y municipales*) for social, environmental, cultural and infrastructure investment.

11

Financial restructuring in Thailand

CHULAKORN SINGHAKOWIN[1]

This chapter considers the current situation of the financial sector in Thailand. I shall limit myself to the impact of our economic crisis on the banking industry and the progress of our response.

1. Source of the crisis

The crisis that broke in 1997 was the product of a lengthy period of over-investment and speculation. The Thai economy had grown at 8 per cent annually for 10 years. Between 1986 and 1997, lending by Thai banks expanded almost 25 per cent per year. Additionally, private sector borrowings from offshore were substantial. In the same period Thailand's main stock index rose 700 per cent, and real estate prices more than quadrupled.

This represented significant productive investment in manufacturing and services. However, it also involved excessive speculation in unproductive assets. The extent of this was made clear in the wake of the crash by sharp asset deflation and widespread overcapacity in the economy. At the end of 2000, the stock index remained at 75 per cent below its peak. There was a 41 per cent vacancy rate in upper-end commercial real estate. Industrial capacity utilization was stagnant at around 58 per cent.

A key to sustaining such a long period of growth and over-investment was the removal of controls on capital account flows in the early 1990s, and the subsequent encouragement of Thai corporations to borrow offshore. The resulting increased inflow of investment and loans helped to overcome a

---

[1] Chairman, Thai Bankers Association; President and CEO, Bank of Asia PCL, Bangkok.

potential domestic capital shortfall that might have slowed economic growth. Nonetheless, there was a financial mismatch. The baht remained closely tied to the dollar, providing investors, lenders and borrowers with false assurances. A floating exchange rate could have helped to moderate excessive capital flows and investment behavior.

Weakness in the Thai economy became apparent in 1996 with a sudden slowdown in growth and the foundering of one commercial bank. This sparked an intense outflow of capital which continued well beyond July 1997, when the baht was delinked from the dollar and devalued. Over the next 12 months the baht fell as much as 55 per cent before it settled at about 36 per cent below its original level.

As capital flowed out of the country and interest rates rose sharply in attempts to restore currency stability, even well-managed, ongoing businesses faced severe liquidity problems. The banking system experienced acute stress due to massive loan defaults. Non-performing loans rose to a peak of 48 per cent of all loans, or 55 per cent of gross domestic product, in May 1989.

2. Rescue and reform

The Thai Government firmly committed itself to a market-led strategy to address this crisis. Although there was significant and useful State intervention and forbearance, efforts were focused on assisting the financial and real sectors to restructure themselves. These efforts included reforms of the laws and institutions for handling insolvency and bankruptcy; creating an agency to assist in debt restructuring; and tax adjustments to enhance the restructuring process.

One almost immediate result was a thinning process in the financial industry. Before 1997, the financial sector comprised 15 Thai commercial banks and nearly 100 non-bank financial institutions, mainly "finance companies", that accounted for almost 30 per cent of the industry.

When the crisis broke, borrower defaults and the liquidity squeeze resulted in the failure of most of the finance companies. Seven of the banks also failed and were nationalized.

The Thai Government moved quickly to staunch panic through a comprehensive deposit guarantee scheme. Simultaneously it forced recapitalization of the remaining financial institutions through regulatory tightening. Full foreign ownership of Thai banks was permitted.

These measures have been generally effective. Today the worst is certainly over. The likelihood of more bank failures is remote.

Recapitalization brought US$21 billion of new funds into the banking sector by the end of 2000. Thirteen commercial banks remained in operation. Four were taken over by foreign banks. Five others were able to obtain new capital privately, as were the remaining finance companies. The rest of the banks remained under government control, with ongoing negotiations to sell one or two of them to foreign investors.

Yet restructuring remained incomplete. The level of bad loans remained at about 30 per cent of all loans, or nearly 40 per cent of gross domestic product. Consequently, banks were still under pressure to increase provisions and could not make new loans. During 2001, we expect total bank lending, 41 months after the crisis broke, to remain flat, or at best show a very modest increase. It is estimated that the Thai banking system may require a further US$10 billion in new capital. However, with such a high level of bad loans, capital cannot be generated internally, and prospective investors have been deterred by the slow pace of loan rehabilitation.

The cause of this deadlock lies in the still-weak legal infrastructure for clearing bad loans. Despite government efforts to reform insolvency and bankruptcy codes and create a special bankruptcy court, the process of clearing bad loans has been sluggish. The laws and court procedures have been insufficient to resolve problem loans or deter new defaults. This has given rise to a culture of non-payment, characterized by so-called "strategic defaulters", where the borrower has the capacity to service debts; however, owing to insufficient legal and social sanction, it feels little obligation to do so. It is estimated that, at their peak, such defaults accounted for nearly 20 per cent of total bad loans.

As a result, banks have been forced to reduce lending and increase provisions, while real sector enterprises are less motivated to strengthen their own balance sheets. This is a crucial challenge to the market-led recovery of the Thai financial sector and the economy as a whole. As long as the process of clearing bad debts progresses very slowly, the issue of capital deficiency remains. Banks are also deterred from making new loans. This constricts the capacity of the economy to resume strong, sustainable growth.

3. Towards further measures

One response to the deadlock in clearing bad loans and fully recapitalizing the banks is the proposal for much deeper intervention by the Government through the creation of a national asset management company, or AMC. The national AMC would purchase bad loans from the banks. This idea was rejected at the beginning of the crisis but gained new momentum in 2000. In the largest government-controlled commercial bank, a dedicated, state-funded AMC has already been created.

There are strong arguments for a national AMC, but it also raises significant issues. It would place an immediate new burden on the national public debt, and arriving at an appropriate purchase price for the assets of the banks requires caution and transparency.

There are also the challenges of moral hazard. With a government agency having taken responsibility for bad loans, the impetus for banking and legal reform is reduced. And if the AMC itself fails to make firm efforts to resolve the bad loans it has taken on, then pressure for reform in the real sector is also lessened.

Beyond this, there are issues of structure and competitive dynamics. In the wake of the crisis, the total number of financial institutions in Thailand has decreased from 120 to 54. Always a sensitive issue, the entrance of very competitive foreign banks into the market through takeovers has been positive without being disruptive.

Arguably, the industry is still burdened with overcapacity and inefficiency. Consolidation might further strengthen the banks. However, it cannot take place without the revision of current regulations, which effectively prevent market-driven mergers and acquisitions.

Should we adhere to current policy, we require further improvement of the market mechanisms for resolving bad loans and completing the restructuring of the financial sector. With a further adjustment of the legal infrastructure to a better-balanced sharing of risk, banks can expedite the resolution of bad loans more quickly and gain the confidence needed for further recapitalization. The deteriorated credit culture can be restored. The banks can then readjust their risk-reward matrix and get on with their role of being the primary motor for economic growth.

12

Lessons for domestic financial policy from the Asian financial crisis

VICTOR B. VALDEPEÑAS[1]

The Asian financial crisis is now an old story . . . now running for four years since its dramatic emergence in mid-1997. But it is a crisis that is far from over. New chapters are still being played out. It is not like the Mexican tequila crisis of 1994 and the Russian economic crisis of 1998, which ended within the year they happened.

As the Asian saga continues, the crisis is turning out to be in many ways different from the old crises of the past. It's a different kind of "animal," so to speak, something we in Asia have never seen before.

The damage is deep and extensive, and the fallout continues. Today, in varying degrees, the economies of Thailand, Indonesia, and the Philippines (TIP) continue to grapple with a huge overhang of corporate bad debts and bankruptcies; this is also true of the Republic of Korea and, to a lesser extent, Malaysia. After three and one half years, economic growth in the TIP countries has remained at around 3 percent, significantly below the 6-8 per cent growth at pre-crisis levels. The currency markets, with Malaysia as the exception, have remained volatile. In 2000, the Philippine peso depreciated by 23 per cent, the Indonesian rupiah by 34 per cent and the Thai baht by 17 per cent versus the United States dollar, putting an additional load on corporate balance sheets that are heavy with foreign debt.

While there has been good progress in 2000 in corporate debt restructuring in Thailand and Indonesia, the non-performing loans (NPLs) of the

---

[1]   President and Chief Operating Officer, UnionBank of the Philippines, Manila.

banking sector have remained high at 22 per cent in Thailand and 30 per cent in Indonesia. In the Philippines, the NPLs rose to 17 per cent. Notwithstanding the great efforts in bank recapitalization and debt restructuring in the region, the number of bank failures and corporate bankruptcies has continued to rise, indicating a problem that will continue to be a noticeable drag on Asia's recovery process.

Worse, after impairing the real economies, the financial crisis is starting to eat into Asia's socio-political stability, magnifying existing distortions and weaknesses at the macro- and microlevels.

What makes the Asian crisis different? The answer: the private sector is at the dead centre of the problem. What we're seeing now is a private sector debt burden that's huge, deep, widespread and unprecedented. At the core of the current crisis is the weak structural framework and risk management infrastructure of the corporate sector that eventually led to a huge debt overhang and balance sheet collapse.

The Asian crisis has been difficult to manage because it was not immediately understood. The extent of the problem was not immediately revealed. The tools were not immediately available to effectively deal with the problem. At the outset, the understanding of the problem was inadequate, and therefore, the analysis and response was inadequate.

Today, three and a half years after the crisis broke out, we're still forming the framework for managing it, at the macro policy level and at the operating or company level. Immediate bailout solutions to deal with future crises are not in place. Restructuring, largely pursued today, takes time because it requires a more detailed and lengthy process involving valuing a company, liquidating its assets, and assessing its operating and organizational structure. This is unlike the balance of payments crisis in the 1980s, for which the solution was largely tried and understood: a macroeconomic, government-to-government bailout.

1. Anatomy of the Asian crisis

Asia's recovery is taking a long time and the process will take a much longer than the country and regional economic crises that the world saw in the 1970s and the 1980s.

This is a result of the many complex issues involved, including the following:

- Repair of the corporate balance sheet;
- Massive overhang of bad debts of both financial institutions and non-financial enterprises, which weakened the financial system;

- A framework, both legal and non-legal, that is still taking shape: asset management companies (AMCs) and new rules such as single borrower limits (SBLs), equity limits, mergers and acquisitions, are still being written;
- Secured versus unsecured lending and asset verification;
- Valuation of collateral;
- Recessionary conditions, excess capacities;
- Heavy damage to the engine of growth—the private sector;
- Losses incurred by depositors/investors;
- Issues of deposit guarantees;
- A variety of unsettled issues.

Prior to the 1990s, country crises had their roots in weaknesses in macroeconomic policies that resulted in balance of payments problems. Such crisises manifested themselves mainly in the balance sheets of the central bank/monetary authority and the public sector. Problems would build up over time until they reached crisis proportions. The immediate solution entailed funding assistance from the International Monetary Fund and, together with that, the conditionalities on the conduct of the country's macroeconomic policies. Specific targets on key economic variables and indicators were then laid out, which involved adjustments of the country's foreign exchange rate to more "realistic" levels along with a more restrictive monetary and fiscal policy.

In those times, the adjustment process involving foreign exchange rate devaluation had a very limited direct and outright impact on the corporate balance sheet. This situation prevailed as a result of foreign exchange regulations that largely restricted the corporate sector from taking significant foreign exchange (FX) exposure in the balance sheet. Similarly, increases in interest rates had limited impact because companies were not highly leveraged.

In sum, before the 1990s, the corporate sector in East Asia was much less vulnerable to currency devaluations and interest rate hikes, since market and price risks embedded in corporate balance sheets were largely limited by the regulatory and financial environment prevailing at the time.

The Asian crisis of 1997 is a different story. The crisis is essentially rooted in an excessive build-up of market risks, notably FX risk, in the corporate balance sheet. These risks remained undetected since they were not tracked by the national monitoring system.

This build-up of risks was a product of several trends and developments that swept East Asia. The 1990s saw a major transformation of East Asia's financial markets. With the policy of foreign exchange, trade and investment liberalization being laid out more firmly, together with a pegged/managed-float FX regime, the globalization of Asia's financial markets took hold rapidly. By the end of 1996, East Asia's financial markets could be characterized by:

- A major presence of foreign institutions in banking and in the equity securities business;
- An enormous increase in the total resources of the banking system, with the growth coming from foreign currency funding;
- Significant increase in portfolio investment of global fund managers in the region;
- Emergence of new funding instruments in foreign currency, both in equity and debt markets.

Clearly, the acceleration of the globalization/liberalization process during the 1990s changed the dynamics of country and financial risks in the emerging markets of Asia. Moreover, the macro indicators of GDP growth, balance of payments, current account, international reserves and related measures looked fundamentally sound, although, specific micro sectors, e.g., the real estate and construction sectors in Thailand and Korea, were already beginning to weaken.

The powder keg phenomenon

Thus, the broad indicators were looking good, but underneath these developments was the emergence of new financial risks in corporate balance sheets that were largely undetected and less understood.

These new risks created a "powder keg" phenomenon, wherein the situation looked fine until a financial event sparked a crisis that quickly developed into a regional contagion.

As this scenario played itself out, equity investors were able to perceive the underlying problems ahead of other market participants. Many of them began to withdraw from the Asian equity markets as early as end 1996, seven months before the FX devaluations in July 1997.

In sum, given the underlying "powder keg" situation, it would take only a spark—by way of FX depreciation—to ignite the reversal of flows and heavy covering of very short positions. When the exchange rates began their rapid depreciation, a heavily exposed private sector ran for cover. To cover themselves in a short period of time for risks that took a longer period of time to accumulate, financial players, particularly from the banking sector, looked for exit mechanisms. Unfortunately, the market was not large enough to accommodate the resulting sudden surge in demand for foreign currency. This added to the severity of the crisis and its contagion.

2. Policy implications

Before coming to policy implications, some points are in order. First, the globalization and internationalization of the financial markets is a process that cannot be reversed. Rather, it will accelerate owing to the rapid advances in information technology and communications and the reduction or removal of cross-border barriers. One doesn't stop globalization just because one wants to avoid taking on new forms of risks. An analogy is that one doesn't eliminate credit risk by not lending.

Second, globalization/liberalization brings with it tremendous benefits. It opens the door for domestic entities, private and public, to access the international capital market for much needed equity and debt financing. At the same time, it provides investment opportunities for foreign investors.

However, the third point is that globalization/liberalization carries with it new kinds of risk—new risks on top of the better understood credit and liquidity funding risks that prudential regulations have focused on.

In my view, the biggest factor behind Asia's financial crisis was the massive build-up of FX exposure in private sector balance sheets across the region. This huge FX exposure, both of the domestic corporate sector as well as the global fund managers, fueled the panic buying of United States dollars against local currencies. The illiquidity of the FX spot markets and the limited supply of US dollars funded out of the international reserves contributed to the region-wide panic.

New risk dynamics

Today's market is vastly different from yesterday's market. The new global economy, with its new instruments and new set of rules, has transformed the risk dynamics of investing and operating.

The first policy implication is thus that we need to understand the new risk dynamics. Knowing the problem is more than half the solution. The present tools of economic analysis are inadequate to understand the new risk. Worse, they could lead to wrong analyses and wrong policy prescriptions, with potentially devastating effects on real economies and real people.

The new realities gave rise to new rules in macroeconomic management. There is a need for new tools, a thorough understanding of the new risk dynamics, and a new risk management architecture to help policy makers manage the process of globalization well.

It is high time to have new analytics, new measures and information tools, new monitoring systems to track these new measures, and new risk management infrastructure, especially in the TIP countries. Specifically, there is a need for a new national monitoring system that tracks, among other things, corporate balance sheets and embedded risks, as well as indicators that are not normally measured today but that are of great importance, such as, the investments and risk exposures of non-residents with investment in the country, the so-called "hot money". There is also a need to augment macro analysis with micro balance sheet analysis. Also, all entities, private sector and government alike, must embrace the discipline of risk management.

International reserves

The level of international reserves, which is a most confidence-sensitive indicator, must be viewed in a broader context. The question to ask is whether a country's international reserves are adequate to cover the new risks.

For a long time, international reserves have been linked with imports and the real sector via the import-cover indicator.[2] International reserves should now be linked with the capital account. This has important implications. To start with, in the light of the emerging importance of capital flows relative to the trade in goods and services, international reserves must be augmented to levels that provide extra protection from the adverse effects of sudden reversals in capital flows.

Exit mechanisms: liquidity in emergencies

Exit mechanisms from a crisis are available to governments in the form of standby facilities from international agencies like the International Monetary Fund and the World Bank. Similar exit mechanisms are not available to the corporate sector. Quick-response mechanisms—in terms of funding assistance and standard procedures to deal with weakening balance sheets before they lead to a collapse—are still absent today. Looking back, during the first days of the crisis, central bank and government responses took a long time to materialize, which exacerbated the condition of the corporate sector.

It is a fact that, in times of crisis, access to private capital and debt financing is naturally difficult as financial institutions try to protect themselves first and thus hesitate to take more risks. Given the tightness of the spot markets under such conditions, the hedge markets play a very important role as a non-institutional source of liquidity. There is a need to develop expeditiously the hedge markets and instruments in East Asia, and to strengthen institutional arrangements. As a specific case, monetary authorities today tend to

---

[2]   Typically, this is expressed as the number of months imports that could be purchased with official reserve holdings. – Eds.

restrict the granting of licences to deal in derivative instruments. There is a need to fast-track this process.

Hedge and capital market development

Today, East Asia's hedge markets, especially in the TIP countries, remain in the infancy stage, and therefore the capability to spread risks via hedge instruments remains limited. As hedge markets and instruments remain underdeveloped, hardly understood by investors and institutions alike, corporate exposures in the debt and currency markets will always be vulnerable to risks.

Hedge market liquidity is lacking because the infrastructure is unavailable and knowledge of the way hedge instruments and their markets work is insufficient. The regulatory framework for hedge markets is also underdeveloped. Policies promoting a better understanding of foreign exchange and money market risks and the available hedge products are not in place today.

Clearly, there is a need to introduce new instruments in the market to relieve the FX market of undue stress. Specifically, we may have to explore the use of non-deliverable forwards (NDF) to augment the hedging mechanism in the marketplace. Also, we may have to explore the use of local currency in meeting hedging requirements in order to alleviate the pressure on the FX market. There is also a need to strengthen institutional arrangements to spread out the risks.

The domestic capital markets of the TIP countries—although Thailand has shown improvement since 1999—were too underdeveloped to take up the slack in bank lending. Aside from being an alternative to banks, a liquid and deep domestic debt market is needed to reduce reliance on foreign currency and short-term borrowing—both of which were key factors in the financial turmoil. Policy makers need to address the lack of secondary market liquidity and hedging tools, as well as strengthen the regulatory infrastructure, among other steps.

Extraordinary measures for speculative surges

Extraordinary measures must be resorted to during extraordinary times, on a temporary basis. This may mean a reversal of some liberalization policies in situations of market failure, such as when the markets are not being allowed to clear effectively and efficiently via the forces of demand and supply. The goal is to control speculative demand. Specifically, monetary authorities may tighten FX management and disallow purchases of foreign currency for any other purpose than meeting important underlying obligations for trade and capital transactions.

3. Conclusion

The Asian financial crisis of 1997 was much different from the previous crises. The problem involved more complex, deep-seated weaknesses of the corporate sector that eventually led to balance sheet collapse. These were on top of some policy weaknesses.

Current policy reforms are focusing on solving the debt problem and extricating the private sector and the economy out of their sorry state. Some policies on improving corporate governance and transparency are already underway via legislation in the financial sector. Other important issues like quality of economic growth, quality of information, accounting standards and practices, are also the subject of reforms in Asia.

The crisis highlighted not only the benefits of globalization and liberalization but also the emergence of new kinds of risk. These risks must be understood, monitored and managed for the globalization process to drive progress on a sustainable and stable basis.

13

Liberalization of financial markets: the case for capital controls

MARINA PONTI AND DAVIDE ZANONI[1]

Globalization of the world economy is proceeding at a rapid pace, particularly in the arena of international finance. The presumed virtues of globalization, however, are far from materializing or being fairly distributed among nations. The opening of domestic capital markets to foreign investment is still a relevant component of the "Washington consensus", although many experts argue that the free mobility of private capital in the 1990s was one of the major causes of the financial crises in emerging markets. This chapter argues for partially reversing that opening through "capital controls" operating through financial disincentives (as opposed to administrative prohibitions).

1. Why and how to control flows in developing countries

The liberalization of capital accounts brings equal benefits to both developed and developing countries only theoretically. In practice it leads to increasing benefits for western investors and banks that can take advantage of expanded opportunities for portfolio diversification and the efficient allocation of global savings and investment. It also offers broader investment and risk-diversification opportunities to creditor countries at a time when their ageing populations with growing pension funds seek higher returns on their investments.

A country can take advantage of greater capital mobility only when its domestic financial market is adequately structured. Therefore, while an open capital account is a positive instrument for financially developed countries,

---

[1]   Mani Tese, Italy.

emerging market economies and economies in transition are constantly under threat of being undermined by uncontrolled and unexpected capital flight, as well as by unsound deregulation and liberalization policies. As a result, greater capital mobility brings high costs and limited benefits to countries with emerging markets that lack sound, modern national financial institutions and are vulnerable to the volatility of financial flows.

The financial crises in the 1990s showed that the liberalization process is disastrous when it is not properly managed. Liberalization can be extremely costly and highly dangerous in countries that do not have proper bank regulatory and supervisory structures, well-functioning legal and judicial systems, and adequate safeguards against highly risky and unethical behaviour. Unfortunately, these measures are far from being fully implemented in emerging economies. Despite their importance, such measures are unlikely to be implemented in the near term because of the complex processes involved.

There are temporary measures, however, that can be taken to protect vulnerable national economies from financial instability before strong financial structures are in place. Among others, these include limits on loan-to-value ratios and consumer credit, maximum repayment periods and minimum down-payment percentages. Additional measures that reduce the vulnerability of national financial systems include restrictions on foreign-denominated debt and prudential controls to limit capital inflows.

Chile's experience with capital controls in the 1990s is a concrete example of such a temporary measure. Chile introduced restrictions on capital inflows in June 1991. Initially, all portfolio inflows required a 20 per cent reserve deposit with no interest at the Central Bank. For investment with maturities of less than one year, the deposits applied for the duration of the inflow, except for a minimum stay of 90 days, while for longer maturities the reserve requirement was for one year. In July 1992, the rate of the reserve requirement was raised to 30 per cent, and the holding period was set at one year, independently of the length of the flow.[2] The results achieved by the authorities with this policy have been:

- a decrease in the volume of short-term inflows and an increase of longer maturities. As shown in table 1, the reduction in shorter-term flows was fully compensated by equivalent increases in longer-term capital inflows. Thus, aggregate capital inflows to Chile were not decreased by capital controls;

---

[2]   Medium-term investors were given the option of paying the Central Bank the financial equivalent of the interest foregone by actually leaving funds on deposit for one year. — Eds.

Table 1. Capital inflows (gross) to Chile
(Millions of United States dollars)

Year	Short-term flows	Percentage of total	Long-term flows	Percentage of total	Total	Deposits[a]
1988	916 564	96.3	34 838	3.7	951 402	-
1989	1 452 595	95.0	77 122	5.0	1 529 717	-
1990	1 683 149	90.3	181 419	9.7	1 864 568	-
1991	521 198	72.7	196 115	27.3	717 313	587
1992	225 197	28.9	554 072	71.1	779 269	11 424
1993	159 462	23.6	515 147	76.4	674 609	41 280
1994	161 575	16.5	819 699	83.5	981 274	87 039
1995	69 675	6.2	1 051 829	93.8	1 121 504	38 752
1996	67 254	3.2	2 042 456	96.8	2 109 710	172 320
1997	81 131	2.8	2 805 882	97.2	2 887 013	331 572

Source: Central Bank of Chile.

a Deposits in the Central Bank of Chile due to reserve requirements.

b – indicates that the item is not applicable.

- a decrease in the country's vulnerability to international financial instability;
- an increase in the ability of the Central Bank to implement an independent monetary policy (despite the presence of managed exchange rates) and to maintain a high differential between domestic and international interest rates.

This example shows that temporary measures such as restrictions on capital flows have been useful instruments to help safeguard financial stability, prevent financial crises and encourage long-term capital inflows.[3] Thus, capital controls can be considered as valid, safe and valuable policy options for developing countries.

In the United Nations Secretary-General's report to the Preparatory Committee for the High-level International Intergovernmental Event on Financing for Development (FfD), which will take place in Mexico in March 2002, capital controls are mentioned in paragraph 21 as a temporary measure to protect national stability. The wording underlines, however, that capital controls should not replace the implementation of adequate reforms in the

---

[3]   Following the Asian financial crisis and scarcity of financial inflows, the deposit requirement was reduced to 10 per cent and then zero. — Eds.

financial system. We support this argument, although we reiterate that such reforms are far from being implemented in most emerging markets. Meanwhile the international community should recommend and support immediate measures to protect national financial stability.

Furthermore, the so-called "policy trilemma"—the impossibility of achieving free capital mobility, a pegged exchange rate and an independent monetary policy simultaneously—is a false problem. There is no valid argument or evidence to support the need for full liberalization of capital markets and flows at all cost. On the contrary, ad hoc measures to control capital flows, specifically designed and implemented for each individual country, should be pursued by national governments and strongly encouraged by international institutions.

For an effective capital control policy, one must analyse the composition of financial flows to and from a country and their ability to support its development. In the last two decades, the combination of liberalization, speculation and technological innovation has given rise to a system of huge dimensions, which responds more to rumour than economic fundamentals. The main players in this system, inter alia, commercial and investment banks, exchange (almost) US$2,000 billion daily in currency transactions, and in exchange-traded and over the counter transactions (OTC) in currency derivatives. The vast majority of these transactions are between the major industrialized country currencies. However, even a tiny redirection of such activity to a developing country market would be highly destabilizing. In other words, an additional argument in support of capital control measures is the acknowledgement of the speculative nature of a significant proportion of global financial flows. Moreover, the currency market has grown. According to estimates of the Bank for International Settlements, foreign exchange transactions increased from US$18.3 billion a day in 1977 to almost US$1,500 billion in 1998.

2. The case for global controls

The argument can be taken a step further to a consideration of capital controls more universally and in particular in developed countries. Capital controls can, as the Chilean case showed, allow governments to welcome long-term investments and discourage short-term ones by making them more costly. At the global level as well, capital controls might help shift financial resources, from speculation back into productive and long-term investments.

In addition, the gargantuan dimensions of daily transactions in the currency markets seriously affect the capability of central banks in even the richest countries to react to speculative attacks. Global central bank reserves amount to no more than what is traded in one day of currency transactions on global markets, according to the Bank for International Settlements.

Thus, the volume of short-term capital flows, in particular massive potential inflows and outflows of speculative capital (spot transactions) can lead to substantial exchange rate instability if currency markets are left to themselves, while central banks do not have sufficient financial resources to fight off speculative attacks. Traditionally, a central bank buys and sells its national currency on international markets to keep the currency's value relatively stable. For example, the bank buys its own currency when a glut caused by an investor sell-off begins to reduce the currency's value. In the past, central banks had reserves sufficient to offset most sell-offs or attacks.[4] Currently, speculators have larger pools of cash than all the world's central banks together. This means that many central banks are unable to protect their currencies, and when a country cannot defend the value of its currency, it loses control of its monetary policy.

The international community should address adequately this new situation and design new rules and institutions capable of guaranteeing stability and more equitable growth in the system. The International Conference on Financing for Development (FfD) represents an opportunity to promote a constructive dialogue on these issues among the different actors: governments, United Nations agencies, international financial institutions including the World Trade Organization, civil society and the private sector. The agenda for the meeting contains most of the major current challenges, including domestic resources for development, private financial flows, trade, official development assistance, debt and the international financial architecture.

During the preparatory process and the FfD conference itself, civil society will monitor the decisions made. If these decisions are not adequate, another precious opportunity will be lost. In particular, a consistent discussion of the implementation of a currency transaction tax (CTT) should be held in the context of this conference, which can be a form of capital control. A study of the CTT was recommended by the United Nations General Assembly Special Session on Social Development in Geneva in June 2000.

---

[4]   In fact, even with administrative controls on capital transactions before the breakdown of the Bretton Woods system in 1971, major country central banks could not defend individually against the most severe currency disturbances and thus established the Group of 10 to lend each other reserves in the event of crises. — Eds.

3. The two-tier tax as circuit breaker

Civil society and academics from many countries have already produced studies on the economic feasibility of currency transaction taxes. Currency transaction taxes are uniform international taxes payable on all spot transactions involving the conversion of one currency into another, in both domestic security markets and foreign exchange markets. They would discourage speculation by making currency trading more costly. The volume of short-term capital flows would decrease, leading to greater exchange rate stability.

Achieving this stability through taxation would require high rates, however, and this would seriously obstruct the workings of international financial markets. A small charge on international financial transactions would not create distortions, but neither would it inhibit speculative behaviour in foreign exchange markets. One possible compromise, suggested by Paul Bernd Spahn, Professor at the University of Frankfurt, would be a two-tier structure: a minimal rate transaction tax and an exchange surcharge that, as an anti-speculation device, would be triggered only during periods of exchange rate turbulence. The minimal rate transaction tax would function on a continuing basis and raise substantial, stable revenues without impairing the normal liquidity function of world financial markets. It would also serve as a monitoring and controlling device for the exchange surcharge, which would be administered jointly with the transaction tax. The exchange surcharge, which would remain dormant as long as foreign exchange markets operated quietly, would function as an automatic circuit breaker and go into effect whenever a speculative attack against the protected currency occurred.

A minimal charge during normal times of, for example, 0.02 per cent on foreign exchange transactions would not raise the cost of capital significantly and would probably have no effect on the volume of transactions involving currency conversions. The exchange surcharge, on the other hand, would give the country's monetary authorities an alternative to other monetary policy measures it could take that have such negative effects as sacrificing valuable international reserves or offering excessively high interest rates to retain funds in the country at great expense to domestic enterprises. It would help eliminate expectations of recurrent bailouts by central banks and reduce unethical behaviour and the impact of financial crises.

To summarize, the implementation of currency transaction taxes would:

- reduce short-term speculative currency and capital flows;
- enhance national policy autonomy;

- restore to individual countries taxation capacity eroded by the globalization of markets;
- distribute tax pressures more equitably among different sectors of the economy;
- trace movements of capital to fight tax evasion and money laundering.

In addition, if applied globally, currency transaction taxes could collect substantial resources that could be used for development purposes. The revenues generated should not, however, replace the fulfilment of fundamental commitments, such as the internationally agreed level of official development assistance, adequate debt reduction and cancellation initiatives, and more equitable trade agreements.

Civil society will work hard to make this conference a concrete success. Our overall objective is the definition—in a participatory and transparent process—of new rules for an international financial system based on a more equitable redistribution of benefits and costs. Redistribution should be the core of the political agenda for this conference, as it should be for the new millennium, so that we can reach social and economic development for all.

Part Four:

PROPOSALS FOR MAJOR INTERNATIONAL INITIATIVES

14

Rethinking and recommitting to official development assistance

JENS MARTENS[1]

A broad consensus exists among the development community that official development assistance (ODA) continues to be of vital importance for many countries in the South. ODA is just one of several financial instruments to fight poverty and to promote sustainable development. ODA cannot be a substitute for other necessary actions, such as further debt cancellation, improved trade conditions for developing countries or reforms in the international financial system. It is also an undisputed fact that by far the major share of funds for development purposes has to be raised by mobilizing domestic resources, both of government and private origin. Under clearly defined conditions, private capital flows can also make a positive contribution to development.

Nevertheless, the transfer of public resources has to play an important role because in central areas of sustainable development simple blind faith in private capital and the forces of the free market alone would lead to damaging or at best ineffective results. This is the case, for instance, in the areas of social security, health, education, cultural development, environmental protection and civil conflict prevention. The provision of such national and global public goods by governments and international organizations will, in the future, probably require far more official funding than has so far been made available.

---

[1] Member of the Executive Board of World Economy, Ecology and Development (WEED), Germany.

1. The crisis of ODA

It is no exaggeration to say that official financing for development is in a serious crisis. The most visible sign of this crisis is the continued downward trend in official development assistance in recent years. Net ODA by the developed countries fell from a previous high of US$59.2 billion in 1994 to US$53.1 billion in 2000, and its share in gross national product accordingly fell from 0.30 to 0.22 per cent. Since in the same period, private net capital flows rose significantly, the ODA share in the overall resource flows from the North to the South fell to a scant 20.7 per cent in 1999. This marks a remarkable shift in importance from official to private capital flows.

Inadequate responses by donor countries

The governments of the donor countries are trying to compensate for the cuts in their development resources mainly in three ways. First, they are concentrating their efforts on a small set of International Development Targets, in particular the target of halving the share of people living in absolute poverty—defined as living on less than US$1 a day—by the year 2015. However, the question remains as to how these targets can be achieved without clearly quantifying their cost and providing the necessary resources. The notion that raising the effectiveness of ODA can overcome the effect of the cuts in development assistance budgets is completely misleading.

Second, many governments are reacting to the shortage of resources by concentrating money on selected recipient countries with a "good" policy environment. What is particularly problematic here is that selectivity de facto acts as conditionality. Only those countries that fulfill conditions of good economic policy as it is defined by the donors benefit particularly from development assistance. Alternative economic policy approaches and priorities are eclipsed. Given that the trend towards greater concentration on regions can be observed in the aid of several industrialized countries, there is an added danger that inadequate donor coordination is likely to shower some "model countries" with resources while others are excluded.

Third, governments are trying to balance the shortfall in development funding by greater recourse to "public-private partnerships" (PPPs). In specific cases, this may be eminently sensible, as for example when cooperation with small or medium-sized enterprises results in an increase in technology transfer and improved environmental standards, or when organic farming projects are facilitated that would otherwise be impossible. However, PPPs are not a universal panacea, for they run the risk of neglecting precisely those areas of basic social services and poverty eradication that are of high priority simply because they are not profitable for businesses.

2. Recommendations for boosting ODA

The downward trend in ODA flows over the last decade has been accompanied by a watering down of the definition of ODA and the broadened policy conditions for receiving it. This situation is in stark contrast to the global requirements for poverty eradication and sustainable development. Irrespective of pledges made at earlier world conferences and in summit declarations, fewer and fewer resources are available for development today. They are being tied to more and more conditions and have to be used for a growing number of tasks in an increasing number of countries.

One central challenge that the International Conference on Financing for Development will be facing is thus to reverse these trends and create a fundamentally new political framework for official development assistance. The following aspects ought to be considered in this context:

Clear millennium targets for ODA

The declaration of intent of governments to reach a number of International Development Targets by 2015 remains unconvincing as long as it is not tied to a commitment to provide the corresponding resources. As long as there are no demand-based targets for the necessary transfer of resources, the 0.7 per cent target remains relevant as a political indicator of the donors' solidarity.[2] For this reason, the governments should agree on a time-frame (with time-bound intermediate targets) for the implementation of the 0.7 per cent target within the next 10 years.

However, the level of official resource transfer from the North to the South should not be based on the gross national product of the donor countries but on the actual financial needs of the recipient countries. In the framework of the international anti-poverty campaign, the United Nations should first of all examine what volume of national and international resources would be needed to attain the agreed 2015 targets. New financial targets could then be defined on this basis. Here, estimates of costs for the worldwide provision of the basic social services are good reference points.

Further boosting effectiveness of ODA

As already noted, donors have taken steps to try to improve the effectiveness of their assistance. However, much more can be accomplished if the de facto dominance of the donors in designing development projects and programmes,

---

[2] First adopted in 1970, the target is for each donor government to supply ODA equivalent to 0.7 per cent of its gross national product — Eds.

as well as the influence they exercise by constantly posing new conditions, is overcome once and for all. The governments and the people of the developing countries have to gain ownership of their development strategies. In practice, for the governments this also means that they have to shift increasingly from project to programme and budget financing. In this context, the setting up of common pools ought to be examined in the framework of the International Conference on Financing for Development. In this approach, the donors pay the funds for a country into a common pool from which the respective government draws in accordance with the development priorities that it has defined in close consultation with the population. This would mean abandoning donor control of projects and detailed conditionality.

If the cost of restructuring debt, including ODA loans, is considered a part of the cost of the aid programmes themselves, it is clear that there is room to raise the efficiency of donor transfers. In order to break through the vicious circle of indebtedness, debt relief and new debts, in the future official development assistance, as a rule, ought to be provided in the form of grants. This applies in particular to all investment expenditure that yields neither an adequate profit nor sufficient foreign currency. This would, above all, affect basic social services, environmental protection measures, capacity-building and agricultural production that is not for export purposes.

3. A Global Development Partnership Agreement

The notion of "development aid" was always a misleading euphemism that reduced the cooperation between sovereign States to charitable or even paternalistic relations between donors and recipients. The International Conference on Financing for Development could pave the way towards a more balanced relationship between North and South on the intergovernmental level. In order to overcome, at least in part, the traditional dependency relationship, new forms of contractual relations between North and South should be developed. In spite of its shortcomings, the new Cotonou Agreement (the partnership agreement between the European Union and the associated African, Caribbean and Pacific countries) ought to be mentioned in this context. An agreement of this kind at the global level would raise the reliability of pledges to grant official assistance, making development planning easier in the countries of the South.

In the long term, binding arrangements for a quasi-automatic transfer of resources could be made, perhaps in the shape of a global country financial offset, the level of which would be based on commonly defined development indicators that could replace the unilateral definitions of performance by the donors. At first glance this proposal seems to be utopian. However, there are already precedents of such an "institutionalized solidarity" on national and regional levels. In Germany, for instance, under the concept of financial adjustment among the federal states—the so-called "state financing offset"—billions of dollars are transferred from the economically stronger to the weaker regions each year. The European Union, to name another example, has the instrument of structural funds to support the poorer regions and weaker economic sectors within the Union. By these means, between 2000 and 2006 an estimated 28 billion euros per year (about US$24 billion per year) will flow from the richer to the poorer sectors and regions of the EU.

Separate and additional funds for global public goods

Adequate financing of "global public goods" (such as protection of the rainforests, the seas, and the ozone layer, and the prevention of communicable diseases) is crucial to the survival of humankind. However, the funds required here should not be taken out of the budget for official development assistance, since this would represent a further reduction in the already scarce resources available for development tasks in the narrower sense. Global public goods ought to be financed by new and additional means; statistically, these new means should be recorded separately from ODA. Mobilizing these funds would be accomplished both via the national budgets of the respective responsible ministries (environment, health, research and education) and via new international financing instruments. Here, internationally harmonized taxes and fees could play a special role, particularly proposals for a currency transaction tax (CTT), an international shipping tax, a tax on jet fuel and an international carbon (energy) tax. In this context, raising funds for the replenishment of the Global Environment Facility (GEF) in 2002 is of particular importance.

Strengthening the economic role of the United Nations

The implementation of the proposals outlined above—particularly for a global development partnership agreement and a more reliable transfer of resources—would require a strengthened role of the United Nations. In a genuinely multilateral and participatory system of global development finance, the United Nations (and not the World Bank or the Development Assistance Committee of the Organisation for Economic Cooperation and Development) has to be the main body for decision-making and policy coordination.

The Charter of the United Nations unambiguously states its central role in global macroeconomic policy formulation and guidance. However, it is no secret that in reality the relevant decisions in this field are taken at the summits and meetings of finance ministers of the seven major industrialized countries and the annual meetings of the International Monetary Fund and the World Bank. Athough the International Conference on Financing for Development could be a first step to reverse this trend and to revitalize the mandate of the United Nations in the field of (so-called) "hard" economic issues, other steps must follow. What we need are institutional reforms and a new division of labour between the United Nations, the World Bank and the IMF in the system of global development finance, with the United Nations as undisputed lead agency.

4. Conclusion

In the United Nations Millennium Declaration, the heads of State and Government reaffirmed that solidarity has to be one of the fundamental values which are essential for international relations in the twenty-first century. The Declaration states: "Global challenges must be managed in a way that distributes the costs and burdens fairly in accordance with basic principles of equity and social justice. Those who suffer or who benefit least deserve help from those who benefit most".[3]

If this important commitment is to be realized, it must to be translated into concrete political action. The International Conference on Financing for Development offers the historic opportunity to give a signal of global solidarity. In order to meet this challenge, governments frankly have to move beyond the agreed upon language of the past and to take credible steps towards a real North-South partnership.

---

[3]   United Nations General Assembly resolution 55/2, para.6.

15

A unified programme to bridge the digital divide

RODNEY HARPER[1]

1. The increasing "digital divide"

Emerging economies have the potential to experience significantly higher growth rates than developed economies over the next decade or more, and could account for a major part of global economic growth over this period, depending upon their ability to attract worldwide capital flows. However, there is a widening wealth gap between the North and the South or the developed and the developing worlds, with the latter disadvantaged through poverty, health problems and illiteracy. There is also a widening "digital divide" between North and South, which will become increasingly costly. Internationally unified actions need to be facilitated to reduce the divide, and the United Nations can help.

Alcatel is a global telecommunications and Internet solutions supplier operating in 130 countries worldwide. It has a global perspective on the information and communications technology (ICT) markets, and thus it can see first-hand the increasing digital divide. Over 15 per cent of Alcatel's turnover of 23 billion euros in 1999 came from the developing world. Moreover, Alcatel is present in some 38 or more countries in Africa, is growing strongly in fast-developing markets in Asia and the Pacific and is well-positioned in Latin America.

---

[1]   Director, International Department, Alcatel, France.

The digital divide exists between those with access to information, as represented by the Internet, and those without. Such a divide between those with access to knowledge (mainly in the developed world) and those without (mainly in developing countries), is illustrated by the following:

- 1 out of every 2 Americans is already on-line;
- 1 out of every 250 Africans is online.

Thus some 90 per cent of all Internet users are found in the industrialized countries.

Together with developing country limitations in the provision of basic services and infrastructure, such as the supply of electricity, transportation links, housing, clean water, health care and education, this so-called digital divide, viewed as driven by globalization and the rapid spread of digital technology through the Internet, was also identified as a major concern by the Group of Eight (G8: the major industrialized countries and the Russian Federation) at the meeting in Okinawa in July, 2000. The G8 has, as a result, created the Digital Opportunities Task Force to work on the problem of the digital divide.

Opportunity from ICT and the Internet

Although the Internet can be viewed as a threat in increasing the digital divide, it can also present an opportunity to support sustainable economic growth in developing countries. ICT cannot directly alleviate poverty. However, it can contribute indirectly to development by means of its influence on economic growth as well as its ability to support access through improved communications links to the health care, education and other social services programmes made affordable by sustainable growth in the local economy.

For example, the Internet can allow the typically smaller companies of the developing world to market their goods and services more cost-effectively via the World Wide Web. These activities could be carried out in collaboration with civil society partners such as foundations in order to support market access and/or provide the necessary training plus technical assistance in the development of local businesses. The availability of an efficient communications infrastructure is an important aspect supporting further investment in developing countries.

However, the information services offered should also be accessible to the population at large, tailored to the real needs of local users. They should also take account of local language and literacy constraints. Thus, affordability, local language and literacy constraints can be overcome through use of the shared access, public kiosk or telecentre approach, with assistance to users provided via an attendant operator on a 24-hour basis. The technology can also support the provision and wider accessibility of banking systems, such as microcredit agencies and the government disbursement of social payments, pensions and other State benefits where people live, sparing the beneficiaries the need to walk, sometimes for days, and afterwards perhaps queue for hours to access payment points in the nearest major towns.

To attract foreign investments in such information and communications technology and Internet-related projects, the supported services should be shown to be sustainable, supplied in line with local regulatory requirements and offering an acceptable return versus the risk for investors. The impact of international assistance and technical cooperation programmes in developing countries can also be enhanced when supported by corresponding government strategies and actions at national level.

Unified actions to initiate and develop sustainable ICT projects

To drive the programmes and processes required to deploy a policy for sustainable development supported by ICT, it is proposed that unified action should be developed, under the auspices of the United Nations, which is viewed as a natural facilitator, between governments, the private sector, financial institutions, service/content providers, suppliers and non-governmental organizations, with the objective of identifying, defining, financing, engineering, building and supporting sustainable communications projects in the developing world.

To support such initiatives in the target countries, national policies and strategies would have to be put in place to ensure access to information and communications technologies. Local education and the skills necessary to use these technologies must also be available, so that ICT may serve as an important driver for development and growth in employment. Such investment in human resources, together with ICT capital and its knowledge-based culture, can also offer developing countries the opportunity to "leapfrog" certain stages in traditional economic development should they choose to do so. For example, it would be possible to target the service industry instead of capital intensive, hardware manufacturing when volume-based economies of scale are not apparent. This can follow from strategy and policies at the national level aimed at developing:

- A coherent national ICT strategy;
- An affordable telecommunications infrastructure;
- An educated workforce.

2. Examples of bridging the "digital divide"

Alcatel itself is a member of the private sector-sponsored Global Business Dialogue on Electronic–Commerce (GBDe) and is active within the Digital Bridges Working Group established by GBDe, focusing on the role business can play in helping bridge the digital divide.

In Cambodia for example, Alcatel telecommunications scholarships have already been awarded to more than 40 Cambodian students, as part of a US$50,000 commitment made by Alcatel in the year 2000 to the telecommunications industry in Cambodia. The aim is to help Cambodian youths interested in the industry to pursue their studies by awarding scholarships, as well as by giving additional training to current employees in the industry to upgrade their skills.

Similarly, Alcatel is demonstrating how to bridge the digital divide with a pilot, satellite-based communications project in Mali. This involves Alcatel as the initial technology provider, acting together with partners (for example, for service/content provision and investment) to demonstrate viability and to attract in turn further foreign investment inflows. The project also includes a pilot communications scheme supporting Internet telephony, high-speed file transfer and streaming video services, the latter being important for educational purposes.

The project target is to serve 702 public cyber centres country-wide over the next two years, including 702 schools with dedicated teachers. In addition, the communications services offered are in support of the Government of Mali decentralization process aimed at countering urban drift, which otherwise can tend to overload existing educational, health and other social services in the developing world.

These are modest initiatives that can be built upon.

16

Spreading the capacity for effective demand for finance: a new cooperation framework

TARIQ BANURI AND ERIKA SPANGER-SIEGFRIED[1]

This chapter examines the issue of financing for development from the perspective of the RING of sustainable development institutions, an international network of organizations that undertakes sustainable development policy research and advocacy at global and national levels, with an emphasis on the experiences and perspectives of the local level. The key insight in this chapter is based on a distinction between what we call the traditional "supply-side" approach to financing for development, preoccupied with the mobilization of concessional resources, and an alternative "demand-side" approach that focuses instead on creating capacity to use financial resources effectively, especially on the part of small and medium-scale entities, which should be able to access and deploy financial resources on commercial terms. While the conventional approach is concerned directly with identifying new sources of funds, shoring up existing ones, and encouraging the redirection of others, the alternative proposed here would increase confidence and reduce the risk perceived in alternative-scale investment.

This argument emanates from the experience at local levels in programmes and projects of sustainable livelihoods, poverty eradication and natural resource conservation. Experience shows that, except in situations of dire emergency, support for capacity-building to use resources productively is

---

[1] Senior Research Director and Research Associate respectively, at Stockholm Environment Institute, Boston, and respresentative of the Regional and International Networking Group (The RING)..

far more effective and relevant to sustainable development than the provision of concessional assistance. In the first place, given the existing institutional structure, it is difficult to ensure that concessional assistance actually reaches its target. Second, capacity-building in productive activity is more sustainable in the long run, since it enables access to relatively stable conventional resources rather than unpredictable charitable ones. Third, this approach does not create a culture of dependence, which is inherent in approaches based on charity. Finally, the major conceptual and practical breakthroughs in this regard, including microcredit, came from institutions that sought to enhance access of large numbers of people to credit on market terms rather than offer them unsustainable subsidized credit.[2]

This distinction has become more relevant in the charged atmosphere around discussions of sustainable development. On the one hand, there are growing concerns that the decline in official development assistance (ODA) flows will seriously undermine the prospects for sustainable development. On the other hand, some point with hope and others with anxiety to the dramatic increase in foreign direct investment. Finally, there is a debate over whether development has to be financed mainly from domestic resources, with foreign resources playing a secondary—and, as some argue, often a deleterious—role; or whether the distinction between domestic and foreign resources has blurred in the age of rapid globalization.

The demand-side perspective can provide a framework for assessing and even synthesizing these diverse arguments. Rather than berating developing countries for not raising domestic resources, it focuses on the creation of capacity, legitimacy and effectiveness that will engage both domestic and foreign resources in development-supporting activities. Rather than debate endlessly the relative irresponsibility of private and public flows, it seeks to establish systems that can ensure better accountability and transparency of all such flows. Rather than bemoan the exclusion from financial flows of particular areas of activities (for example, poor communities, long-term programmes and mid-sized projects), it seeks actively to develop institutions that will broaden the access to finance of hitherto excluded sectors. Rather than criticizing rich countries for not sustaining their ODA levels, it seeks to re-establish the legitimacy of responsible ODA among taxpayers in those countries. In other words, this perspective provides an alternative framework for reconciling seemingly irreconcilable positions.

---

[2]   See, in a similar spirit, chapter 1 above on microcredit. – Eds.

As the tenth anniversary approaches of the Earth Summit (United Nations Conference on Environment and Development, held at Rio de Janeiro, Brazil in 1992), the declining trends in many forms of development finance reflect poorly on the global commitment to the goals of Agenda 21. A renewed commitment would involve a three-pronged international agenda:

- Reversal of the trajectory of declining sources of finance;
- Creation of an institutional framework that would enable and encourage private, non-concessional finance to reach small and medium-scale enterprises;
- Strengthening the capacity of small and medium-scale borrowers to access and deploy resources effectively.

We argue here that progress on all three fronts would be rendered more robust and sustainable if the problem were treated not merely as enhancing supply, but as building effective demand.

1. Sustainable livelihoods as a development goal

A central goal for any developing country today, as for any industrialized one, is sustainable development, development that serves to harmonize growth with social and ecological parameters and aims, not only for the protection of rights and conservation of natural resources, but for the eradication of poverty. Of the services provided by finance, what is needed to advance sustainable development and alleviate the plight of the poor is less a handful of expensive, large-scale development projects than large numbers of sustainable livelihoods. These are best created by small, local, eco-efficient enterprises. Helping them to access finance, however, has not been simple.

How, then, is sustainable development to be advanced? Both the literature and development practitioners are converging on a set of complementary principles that can serve to advance this urgent work. According to these principles, human and institutional capacity can create the ability to act, and this ability, when directed towards building sustainable livelihoods, can go far towards realizing the goals of sustainable development. More than job creation, this approach aims at *sustainability*, ecological as well as social and economic. Rather than focus on short-run interventions, sustainable livelihoods programmes start from varying entry points—through social mobilization, credit, technology, policy and governance reform—depending on local conditions and needs, to help the poor to expand their asset base. The approach seeks to enhance the social capital of the poor and their access to natural capital, rather than concentrating solely on income or financial/physical capital. In short, it focuses broadly on livelihoods rather than income or jobs.

While the sustainable livelihoods approach may capture a number of elusive goals for environment and development, it is also to be recommended by its many practical attributes. Most critically, the capacity in many developing countries to absorb more labour in traditional sectors (for example, agriculture) is rapidly reaching a plateau, whereas the sustainable livelihoods approach offers an alternative for widespread job creation.

Recognition of smaller-scale activity

Countries now need to create sustainable livelihoods on a large scale, and to accelerate the rate of growth of their economies. The reasons for failure on these fronts thus far lie, ironically, in the very structure of industrial production that has provided so many benefits for so many people all over the world: its emphasis on mechanization, centralization and large scale; and the use of energy- and material-intensive technologies. There are, of course, sectors for which the economies of scale favour large, mechanized production units, but there are many sectors where economies of scale are not relevant. Most industries producing basic goods for rural populations are commercially viable even at very small scales. And because of the low capital requirements, they can have high returns on investment, in some cases even double those for their larger counterparts. Furthermore, in small and mini-enterprises, the scarce capital is recovered in a much shorter time, making it possible to reinvest in further production and job creation.

Today, there is a widespread recognition in the international development community of the importance of financing small-scale sustainable enterprises in developing economies, although very few mechanisms are yet available at the community level. The availability of grants is dropping, and conventional financing institutions remain inaccessible because smaller-scale sustainable livelihoods projects generally have little collateral to pledge and no track record to demonstrate a steady cash flow. Given the weighty administrative costs and small size of such allocations, and the sparse credit histories and high perceived risk of many borrowers and grant recipients, finance continues to be the missing link to the widespread creation of sustainable livelihoods.

2. Enhancing Demand for Finance

Alternative finance mechanisms are clearly an essential component of effective development policy. However, if they are to be effective, the risk perceived in directing finance through these mechanisms to sustainable development activities must be reduced. The more ambiguous factors are those needed to make such forms of finance viable to lenders and grant-makers, and accessible to users. The important lessons for this effort, however, are no different from those that have emerged from recent development literature and experience: namely, that capacity-building and institutional strengthening lead to greater confidence and support at all levels of development activities.

When applied to the question of development finance, the key and innovative attribute of these methods is that they imply a focus on demand. The reduction in risk and handling costs (essential to successful lending) and restoration of grant-maker confidence (essential to aid) cannot be addressed through changes in supply. Movement on both fronts is central to future sustainable development activities; each must be approached through a strengthening of project efficacy and accountability, and, in the longer term, records of creditworthiness. In other words, risk reduction, efficiency and restoration of legitimacy can only be achieved by strengthening the quality and quantity of the demand for finance.

Capacity-building and institutional strengthening

Numerous alternative finance models exist, such as microcredit, franchising and partnering. Expansion of the use of these alternative instruments—in the process, proving their soundness and utility—is arguably the cornerstone to more effective use of development finance. However, increased utilization of various forms of credit and aid requires an increase in the capacity of recipients and strengthening and support of intermediary institutions.

The notions of building capacity and strong institutions have received significant attention in recent years, mainly in the context of national development and environmental management. It is now widely held that capacity is required to meet a variety of challenges in these domains.[3] While attention has been directed towards capacity-building of the community of non-governmental organizations (NGOs), this effort has not extended the issue of small-scale finance with adequate rigour. Little direct attention has been given to the capacity-building of NGOs to handle and administer this level of development finance, a factor that may have served to slow the evolution of development work in general.[4]

---

[3]   Agenda 21 states, for example, that a "fundamental goal of capacity-building is to enhance the ability to evaluate and address the crucial questions related to policy choices and modes of implementation among development options, based on an understanding of environmental potentials and limits and of needs as perceived by the people of the country concerned".

[4]   It is through the framework of the NGO community, after all, that various target groups—rural populations, ecologically vulnerable groups, the informal sector, women—are most readily accessed, and it is through these groups, then, that small-scale development finance can be most effectively utilized.

Thus, a significant gap exists between the traditional supply-oriented finance framework and the potential users of sustainable development finance—a gap that could be filled by institutions, if they were provided adequate support. As banks are not prepared to serve as the creditor of many small loans, neither will finance reach the necessarily diffuse level of small credit in the form of FDI or even ODA; smaller-scale, intermediary institutions are essential, ones to which modest lines of credit can be extended for subsequent low-cost, mini-credit distribution. The NGO community is well poised to fill this niche, and the development of NGO capacity in this realm could essentially lead to the creation of a supplier network, a small-scale credit market, a project finance monitoring system, and to the support of long-term supplier/purchaser relationships.

In addition to institutions, the capacity of potential borrowers to use finance—from identifying, applying for, spending, accounting for and, in the case of loans, paying back—is a second focus of demand strengthening. The demand for finance to launch small enterprises is thought to be vast. However, this demand does not translate into the capacity to use the money effectively. Nor does the ability to launch a small enterprise mean that it will be a sustainable one. Both require skills, support, marketing channels and access to technology. The two groups—intermediaries and recipients—possess a number of the tools to build and run alternative scale finance and monitoring systems. They do, however, require technical and networking assistance, as well as access to technology and training programmes to do so.

Two factors in particular call for international support of such a capacity-building effort. The first is the large scope of demand for this sort of credit framework—estimated to be in the millions of borrowers in India alone. The second factor is the large potential that can be realized, given existing capacity, through such activities as network building and mutual learning.[5] In short, finance is needed to meet the sustainable development goal of strengthened capacity—of the individual, the community and the institution—and capacity is needed now in order to mobilize and utilize this finance.

Reducing risk and building confidence

Confidence is a cornerstone of development activities, and with its deterioration come a number of impediments to the development process. These impediments tend ultimately to impact the movement of finance. The

---

[5] A third factor may be new international calls for a global grant-making institution on the scale of the World Bank, if not the Bank itself. Though unlikely, a strong renewal in this type of aid could be greatly encouraged by stronger recipient capacity.

approval and release of funding can be obstructed, and finance can be ineffectively disbursed and underutilized; with a breakdown in confidence, the process of financing development activities can fail at a number of points.[5]

In many ways, confidence and risk are related commodities: to the commercial lender, the level of risk determines the viability of a loan; to the supplier of aid, confidence of both the players and the goal itself weighs heavily on funding decisions. Approaching again from the demand side, increased commercial lending requires efforts to reduce risk, just as a reversal of the slump in bilateral grants requires a restoration of confidence in the effectiveness of charitable aid.

This decline in confidence on the part of private lenders and official donors is not unwarranted. However, it comes at a time when real advances in monitoring and accountability have been made in a number of countries. Similarly, empirical studies by the Government of India, the World Bank and others show that among the potential clients for small-scale credit, a significant percentage have high levels of creditworthiness. The paradox of our global economy is that there is virtually no source of funding today that can actually deliver adequate financial credit where it has the greatest potential impact, either on the generation of employment or on national economies. Carefully designed lending programmes can therefore be both financially profitable and socially worthwhile.

3. Conclusion

The credit and aid mechanisms through which sustainable development is most greatly advanced are of multiple scales, the most productive of which can tend, in developing countries, to be quite small. Small-scale potential clients include a wide range of industries, trades and communities capable of "boot-strapping" local, and consequently national, economies. Among these, a large number could contribute to sustainable development by enhancing coping strategies and protecting communities from shocks, by fulfilling basic needs, creating livelihoods, generating purchasing power and conserving natural resources.

The body of projects and enterprises that create sustainable livelihoods can grow rapidly provided a systematic infrastructure is built up to provide

---

[5]   At a bilateral or multilateral level, trust of the public of the donor countries, the members of a donor foundation, the overseeing agency of the donor government, the public or private recipient agency, and even the financial conduit can be lost. Domestically, the generation of development finance can be hindered by government corruption or public disapproval of the use of taxes, and thus of the process of tax collection itself.

them the needed support. Both the tenets of the Earth Summit and the conventional wisdom on development call for action in this direction. Successful models exist that can be readily replicated, yet real action on the ground remains limited. In its response to the questions of future development finance, the international community would be well advised to encourage these alternatives, and to place the development of this type of framework and the capacity of participant groups at the centre of its strategy.

17

Required international initiatives in trade policy

TOM NILES[1]

This chapter concerns the ways in which trade and the continued liberalization of the rules for international trade can contribute to development. The phenomenon of donor fatigue is a very important point to keep in mind when we think about where the resources are going to come from for the development of less developed countries. Certainly, if you look at the role of the United States of America, just to take one case of development assistance, I think we're down now to 0.17 per cent of our gross domestic product in overseas development assistance (ODA). Regardless of whether a Democrat or a Republican occupies the White House, I can fearlessly predict that that figure will not go up. I believe that other donor countries in Western Europe, as well as Japan, are also suffering from what we call "donor fatigue". As a result, development funds from official sources and also from the international financial institutions, which depend to a substantial degree on the developed countries for their resources, will remain limited and insufficient for the needs. So, increased exports and enhanced flows of direct foreign investment, in my view, are the two key factors if we are to achieve development in the developing countries.

1. Developed country trade policy

By and large, the developed countries—my own country, the United States, Canada, the European Union and Japan—have talked a better game than they have played on the trade issue. We did take steps in the Uruguay

---

[1]   President, United States Council for International Business, New York.

Round of multilateral trade negotiations to give, or to try to give, the developing countries what was referred to as "special and differential treatment", and to a degree that succeeded. Today, however, the developing countries in the World Trade Organization (WTO) are dissatisfied with the results of the Uruguay Round, and not without reason. One of the problems that the World Trade Organization faces today is that the implementation of the Uruguay Round agreement by many of the developing countries, now over five years after the agreement went into effect, is lagging. This is due in part to their dissatisfaction with the results of the negotiations.

In 1984, the United States and other developed countries adopted a system of tariff preferences—the Generalized System of Preferences (GSP)—which were designed to assist the developing countries. To a certain degree, these preferences have proven useful, particularly for the more developed among the developing countries. Basically, however, if you look at GSP in the United States, and also in Japan and Western Europe, these programmes have been structured so as to exclude those product areas in which the developing countries are the most competitive, particularly light industrial products, textiles and footwear, apparel and yarn, and agriculture. If we are serious about using trade as a key element in development, we must be prepared to expand significantly the list of products from the developing countries that can receive free and unhindered access to the markets in Japan, the United States and the countries of Western Europe.

So, if we are serious about using a new multilateral trade round as a development tool, we really have to take on board the problem of access to developed country markets by developing country products in areas such as textiles, apparel and yarn, footwear and agriculture. This will require political leadership.

It will take tremendous political leadership on the part of the leaders of developed countries—particularly the European Union, Japan and the United States—because, among other things, we in the United States will have to dismantle a substantial part of our agricultural protection in areas such as sugar, peanuts, cotton and tobacco. The European Union will have to take the same sort of steps with respect to its Common Agricultural Policy (CAP). At the same time, our countries will have to resist what will be very strong pressures from domestic interests to derogate from the phase-out of the Multifibre Arrangement, which was agreed during the Uruguay Round.[2] One of the ways

---

[2]   The "Arrangement regarding International Trade in Textiles" covered textile trade from 1974 to 1994. Since 1995, the Agreement on Textiles and Clothing governs a ten-year phase out of the earlier discriminatory practices — Eds.

in which the developing countries did not receive real "special and differential treatment" in the Uruguay Round is that the phase-out of the Multifibre Arrangement was "back-loaded". It began, to be sure, on 1 January 1995, but for the first five years the concessions were relatively limited and the real phase-out occurs towards the end of this period. Now, there will be great pressures in this country, Japan and Western Europe to derogate from the phase-out of the Multifibre Arrangement. If governments do not show political leadership and resist these protectionist pressures, the developing countries will be deprived of this opportunity, for which they paid in the Uruguay Round agreement.

The Commissioner for External Trade of the European Union, Pascal Lamy, announced in late 2000 that the European Union was going to eliminate all tariffs and quotas for imports from the 48 least developed countries to the European Union, except for arms. That is a heroic pledge on the part of the Commissioner. The European Union reached an agreement on a modified form of that pledge in time for the Third United Nations Conference on the Least Developed Countries in May 2001. It is also somewhat back-loaded, particularly in sensitive agriculture goods. I wish the European Union luck because, should it succeed, it would involve the partial removal of the CAP, which has been a major impediment to the development of international trade for many years.

In the United States, we have agricultural programmes that are only slightly less iniquitous than those of the European Union. Our sugar programme, for instance, raises the domestic price of sugar roughly three times over the world market price. It poses a very heavy penalty on the many in order to benefit the few who raise sugar in this country. It also has very bad environmental consequences for the United States, and it deprives the developing countries of a large market. You would think that this programme would have been abolished long ago, but it hasn't been because this would be politically difficult to do in the United States. So, we have some important things to do in this country, which I think will require great political leadership.

One final point I would make about trade is that we have to keep in mind that the full phase-out of the Multifibre Arrangement will create a very interesting dynamic among the exporting countries, namely one in which it is possible for China to end up with the largest part of this market, taking markets away from other developing countries that have succeeded in developing their exports to Western Europe and the United States.

One positive thing I might note in case of my own country is the adoption of the Trade and Development Act of 2000 by our Congress in May 2000.

The Act, which includes the African Growth and Opportunity Act and the United States-Caribbean Basin Trade Partnership Act, is a very interesting Bill because it essentially goes beyond GSP. It takes the Generalized System of Preference as its basis and adds access to the United States markets in areas previously excluded from GSP, notably agriculture and textiles. So, in the United States we have taken the first important step in the direction of opening up our markets and indeed giving the developing countries what they were pledged to receive in the Uruguay Round, "special and differential treatment".

2. Foreign direct investment policy

Let me just add a word about direct foreign investment. If you look at the way private direct investment flows in the world economy today, it is mainly comprised of companies from developed countries investing in other developed countries. Seventy-five per cent of the direct foreign investment is between developed countries. Although there are pools of resources here available to investors, they are not going to invest in countries where you don't have an honest government, an honest system of laws and regulations, and an honest system of corporate governance. So if the developing countries are really seriously interested in attracting direct foreign investment, the way forward is very clear. It is through adopting measures such as the Principles of Corporate Governance of the Organisation for Economic Cooperation and Development (OECD). The OECD has issued a handy pamphlet that contains those principles. It is also essential to sign up to the OECD Anti-Bribery Convention. These are two absolutely key elements if the flow of direct capital investment is to be partially redirected away from developed markets into markets in the developing countries.

18

Tax competition and tax havens

JENNY KIMMIS AND RUTH MAYNE[1]

Tax havens and offshore financial centres (OFCs) have seldom figured as prominently in media coverage of economic affairs as they do today. Interest has focused on the concerns of northern governments and the interests of powerful transnational corporations (TNCs). The main actors in the debate are revenue authorities, corporate lawyers, tax accountants and financial journalists. By contrast, the world's poorest countries are conspicuous by their absence. This is unfortunate because offshore tax havens represent an increasingly important obstacle to poverty reduction. They are depriving governments in developing countries of the revenues they need to sustain investment in basic services and the economic infrastructure upon which broad-based economic growth depends. This chapter argues that offshore centres are part of the global poverty problem and that the interests of the poor must be brought onto the reform agenda.

1. Losses to developing countries

It is impossible to calculate the financial losses to developing countries associated with offshore activity. Secrecy, electronic commerce and the growing mobility of capital have left all governments facing problems in revenue collection. The borderline between tax evasion and tax avoidance is becoming increasingly blurred. But at a conservative estimate, tax havens have contributed to revenue losses for developing countries of at least US$50 billion a year. To put this figure in context, it is roughly equivalent to annual aid flows to

---

[1]   Oxfam (Great Britain) Policy Department, United Kingdom.

developing countries. We stress that the estimate is a conservative one. It is derived from the effects of tax competition and the non-payment of tax on flight capital. It does not take into account outright tax evasion, corporate practices such as transfer pricing, or the use of havens to under-report profit.

Revenue losses associated with tax havens and offshore centres cannot be considered in isolation. They interact with problems of unsustainable debt, deteriorating terms of trade, and declining aid. There is no doubt that the human development costs of tax havens are large. The US$50 billion loss is equivalent to six times the estimated annual costs of achieving universal primary education, and almost three times the cost of universal primary health coverage. Of course, ending the diversion of resources from governments into corporate profit margins and offshore bank accounts provides no guarantee that the funds released will be used for poverty reduction purposes. This will depend on governments' developing effective poverty reduction strategies. However, allowing current practices to continue will undermine the successful implementation of such strategies.

The extent of offshore financial activity is not widely appreciated. The globalization of capital markets has massively increased the scope for offshore activity. It is estimated that the equivalent of one third of total global output is now held in financial havens. Much of this money is undisclosed and untaxed, and the rest is under-taxed. Governments everywhere have become increasingly concerned at the implications. In Great Britain, the Government's efforts to prevent the use of tax havens to under-report profit (and hence tax liability) has brought it into conflict with powerful transnational companies. At least one major corporation has responded by threatening to relocate its investments from Great Britain. Such problems have lead to a proliferation of initiatives designed to tackle various aspects of the problem. The Organisation for Economic Cooperation and Development (OECD) is leading an initiative to crackdown on harmful tax competition. United Nations agencies are trying to curb money laundering and the Financial Stability Forum (FSF) is examining the impact of the offshore system on global financial stability.

These initiatives are useful up to a point, but they primarily reflect the concerns of northern governments. Ironically, these governments are in a far stronger position than their counterparts in developing countries. If revenue authorities in Great Britain and Germany feel threatened by offshore activity, how much more severe are the problems facing countries with weak systems of tax administration? And if governments in rich countries see tax havens as a threat to their capacity to finance basic services, how much more serious are the threats facing poor countries? After all, these are countries in which 1.2

billion people have no access to a health facility, in which 125 million primary school-age children are not in school, and in which one out of every five people lives below the poverty line.

Lack of attention to poverty is only one part of the problem with current initiatives. Another is their lack of balance. Some developing country havens justifiably see the actions of northern governments as being unbalanced and partial. Financial havens are part of a much wider problem that extends beyond the "offshore" activity of small island States to "onshore" activity in major financial centres such as the City of London and New York. Yet OECD efforts to address harmful tax competition have involved a crackdown on small State financial havens, while a far more light-handed approach has been applied to member countries engaging in harmful tax practices.

2. Channels of the loss to development

Tax havens may seem far removed from the problem of poverty, but they are intimately connected. There are three major ways in which offshore centres undermine the interests of poor countries.

Tax competition and tax escape

Tax havens and harmful tax practices provide big business and wealthy individuals with opportunities to escape their tax obligations. This limits the capacity of countries to raise revenue through taxation, both on their own residents and on foreign-owned capital. This can seriously undermine the ability of governments in poor countries to make the vital investments in social services and economic infrastructure upon which human welfare and sustainable economic development depends. It also gives those TNCs that are prepared to make use of international tax avoidance opportunities an unfair competitive advantage over domestic competitors and small and medium-sized enterprises. Tax competition, and the implied threat of relocation, has forced developing countries to progressively lower corporate tax rates on foreign investors. Ten years ago, these rates were typically in the range of 30-35 per cent, broadly equivalent to the prevailing rate in most OECD countries. Today, few developing countries apply corporate tax rates in excess of 20 per cent. Efficiency considerations account for only a small part of this shift (as witnessed by the widening gap between OECD and developing country rates), suggesting that tax competition has been a central consideration. If developing countries were applying OECD corporate tax rates their revenues would be at least US$50 billion higher. If used effectively, funds siphoned through tax loopholes into offshore financial centres could be used to finance vital investments in health and education. None of this is to argue for a return to high tax regimes that deter investment activity. Foreign direct investment has the potential to generate real benefits for development. However, without reasonable levels of tax collection, governments cannot maintain the social and economic infrastructure needed to sustain equitable growth.

Money laundering

The offshore world provides a safe haven for the proceeds of political corruption, illicit arms dealing, illegal diamond trafficking, and the global drug trade. While some havens, such as the Channel Islands and the Cayman Islands, have introduced anti-money-laundering legislation, the problem remains widespread. Havens facilitate the plunder of public funds by corrupt elites in poor countries, which can represent a major barrier to economic and social development. It has been estimated that around US$55 billion was looted from Nigerian public funds during the Abacha Government. To put the figure in perspective, that country is today blighted by an external debt burden of US$31 billion. Northern governments justifiably press Southern governments to adopt more accountable and transparent budget systems, but then create incentives for corruption by failing to deal effectively with tax havens and other tax loopholes.

3. Financial instability

The offshore system has contributed to the rising incidence of financial crises that have destroyed livelihoods in poor countries. Tax havens and OFCs are now thought to be central to the operation of global financial markets. Currency instability and rapid surges and reversals of capital flows around the world became defining features of the global financial system during the 1990s. The financial crisis that ravaged east Asia in the late 1990s was at least partly a result of these volatile global markets. Following the Asian crisis, the Indonesian economy underwent a severe contraction and the number of people living in poverty doubled to 40 million. In Thailand, the health budget was cut by almost one third. Nearly three years after the outbreak of the crisis, the economies of Thailand and Indonesia continue to struggle under the huge public debt burden that it created.

4. Policy proposals

For meaningful change to happen, the international community needs to adopt a more comprehensive and inclusive approach to the issue of financial havens and harmful tax competition. This chapter does not seek to make detailed policy proposals, but rather puts forward a set of guiding principles and six key policy options that should receive serious consideration by the international community.

Oxfam believes that an international framework for dealing with the effects of financial havens and harmful tax competition should include a poverty perspective; a genuinely inclusive approach fully involving developing countries in discussions; a multilateral approach to what are global problems; and strategies to help small, poor and vulnerable economies to diversify from a reliance on harmful tax practices and to comply with standards to prevent money laundering. The following policy options could be considered by the international community to help poor countries stem tax evasion and reduce the negative impact of tax havens:

- A multilateral approach on common standards to define the tax base to minimize avoidance opportunities for both TNCs and international investors;

- A multilateral agreement to allow States to tax multinationals on a global unitary basis, with appropriate mechanisms to allocate tax revenues internationally;

- A global tax authority to ensure that national tax systems do not have negative global implications;

- Support for the proposal for an international convention to facilitate the recovery and repatriation of funds illegally appropriated from national treasuries of poor countries;

- Standards on payment of taxation in host countries to be added to environmental and labour standards as part of the corporate responsibility agenda. Standards requiring TNCs to refrain from harmful tax avoidance and evasion should be factored into official and voluntary codes of conduct for TNCs and for the tax planning industry;

- A multilateral agreement to share information on tax administration to help countries, especially poorer ones, to stem tax evasion.

19

Currency transaction tax: An innovative resource for financing social development

BART BODE[1]

Taxation is the main source of income for funding national social development (education, health and other public services). At the regional level as in the European Union, it is usually through taxation that States finance their actions aimed to reduce inequalities between countries. At the international level, there is no taxation, although there are global needs. It has been observed that various sources of income linked to international financial activities are not taxed, and yet they generate considerable profit for institutions and business. If one could tax these activities, one could help raise resources for global needs. One proposal is thus to introduce a "currency transaction tax" (CTT).

1. What kind of currency transaction tax are we talking about?

Most of the discussions about a currency transaction tax are based on the proposal originally introduced by James Tobin in 1972. This proposal consisted of levying a tax on transactions in foreign currency markets with the aim of reining in short-term, speculative flows of funds and channelling the majority of capital into long-term investments. Tobin proposed introducing a tax of 0.5 per cent on all speculative transactions. Because he was considering speculation in major country currencies, it had to be a tax imposed worldwide, wherever those currencies were traded. The tax also had to be the same everywhere. Tobin believed that this system would give governments greater autonomy to implement their monetary policy, a major concern at the time he was writing.

---

[1]   Head of the Policy Department of Broederlijk Delen, Belgium.

More than 20 years later, most of the criticisms of any form of currency transaction tax are still addressed to the Tobin proposal. They ignore or dispute the evidence and expertise that have been developed since 1972 and the answers that have been given regarding the shortcomings of the original Tobin tax.

A two-rate tax system

In 1994, Paul Bernd Spahn, Professor of Economics at the University of Frankfurt, wrote a memo as an expert for the International Monetary Fund about taxing financial speculation, based on the original proposal of James Tobin. Spahn developed a proposal on the basis of a two-phase tax:

- a minimum tax (0.01 or 0.02 per cent) that would provide a relatively continuous revenue stream during times of "normal" market behaviour;
- a very heavy tax (50 or even 100 per cent) during a financial crisis.

The latter would aim in effect to act as a circuit breaker to virtually halt trade if a currency was rising or falling too sharply. The idea of a circuit breaker is not new. Such a system is already used on some stock markets (for example, the New York Stock Exchange), to halt trading when the situation becomes overheated. The difference, however, is that the typical circuit breaker administratively stops trading, whereas the Spahn proposal would impose a punishing financial penalty to trades that remain permitted.

The Spahn variant offers a number of advantages over the original Tobin tax. The low tax does not disrupt normal market movements and would provide a predictable revenue. The heavy tax is likely to be an effective tool for hindering excessive speculation and thus reduce the extent of crises like the one in South-East Asia in 1997.

Taking the point of view that we wish to generate revenue and avoid crises, the Spahn variant is very attractive. Furthermore, this option is much more feasible politically because both market economists and policy makers see it as realistic. The tax would provide an instrument for tracking market movements (based on data on tax collections) and enable governments to take the necessary measures to change policy before pressures build up to a major crisis. It is the ideal instrument to create time to act, the very time that governments lacked during the financial crises in the past decade.

This is a feasible tax

A few years ago, economist Rodney Schmidt was commissioned by the Department of Finance of Canada to examine how a currency transaction tax could be applied and monitored. According to Schmidt, on the basis of the electronic networks and daily settlements between large banks in different countries, a currency transaction tax could be applied and monitored perfectly. So far, no one has demonstrated the opposite, and most people agree that his proposal could in fact be implemented effectively.

Provided certain conditions are fulfilled, taxing "wholesale" foreign-exchange transactions at the point of payment is likely to be the most watertight, economically efficient, and transparent method of applying CTT and thus controlling financial movements between currencies. Under these conditions, there is no reason to expect any distorting shifts in financial transactions for the sake of tax-avoidance in response to the controls. If it is desired that the controls should be selective, appropriate rebates can be given subsequently.

The tax might be applied, for example, at a moderate rate over the medium term to reduce capital inflows to a particular currency area; or at a penalty rate in the short term to halt a speculative capital outflow. It might also be imposed for national or international revenue purposes.

The required conditions are these:

- Any monetary authority, other than that of one of the four to six key currencies, can apply controls by this method independently and unilaterally on purchases or sales of its currency, provided it has a modern domestic large-value payment system. This condition is now fulfilled by all the Group of 10 countries, by most of the larger middle-income countries and by some large low-income countries. It can be expected to be fulfilled by others in the near future;
- Controls by this method can be applied on any currency now, provided the monetary authorities of the four to six key-currency countries cooperate to impose them;
- Similarly, a uniform tax at a low rate on wholesale foreign-exchange transactions could be applied across the world for global revenue purposes, provided the key-currency countries cooperated to impose it.

One concern about feasibility is whether there would be opportunities for significant "leakage" of transactions through the "retail" market. This would be discouraged by the higher transaction cost of making small-scale purchases and could also be discouraged by regulatory authorities. In any event, the incentive to avoid the tax will be enhanced if any long-term taxes are imposed at very low rates, taxes for medium-term inflow-control purposes at moderate rates, and any penal rates applied only briefly.

In fact, even taking into account that some small problems remain (for example, on some complex derivative products), one can state that this currency transaction tax is far easier to implement than existing income taxes or the systems of value-added tax (VAT) that are common instruments in Europe and other Western countries.

2. Advantages of the proposed CTT

Most countries can adopt the CTT unilaterally

In debates on the 1972 Tobin proposal, an argument was often made that at the present time we do not have an international institution with the legal power to levy an international tax. In the new proposal, we do not need this at all. It has to be stated very clearly that this is a tax that can be raised by any individual country, other than the key currency countries, provided it has the legal authority to levy taxes.

In Latin America, Chile levied a tax for some time on foreign capital invested in the country that operated something like the CTT tax in mainly discouraging short-term inflows.[2] The IMF publication, *Economic Issues,* of September 1999 reported that by taxing short-term capital, as implemented by Chile, hedge funds and other speculators were discouraged from making a sudden decision to move capital. The managers of hedge funds, who attach a great deal of importance to taking and changing positions with a minimum of cost, are especially sensitive to this type of measure.

A global CTT can raise substantial resources for development

The world's currency markets are highly concentrated in a few major countries. This means that if a CTT should be introduced globally, those countries where these markets are located (Japan, the United Kingdom, and the United States) could suddenly have a very large increase in tax revenue, while countries with small financial markets would generate very little revenue. This suggests that some sort of redistribution mechanism should be established.

Part of the revenue in these markets could be allocated to domestic purposes. For the countries in the South, 100 per cent of the revenue could be used for their own development. Their needs are great enough, whereas resources are scarce. For industrialized countries, one might allocate about 20 per cent of the revenue raised from the tax for social purposes in each individual country. The remaining 80 per cent could be dedicated to development cooperation. In such a scenario, a tax of 0.01 per cent would double official development assistance.

---

[2]   This experience is described in chapter 13 above. — Eds.

The United Nations, in collaboration with IMF and the World Bank, could establish an international agreement on redistributive measures if such a currency transaction tax were to be introduced. This agreement could feature the exact methods to be used regarding application, monitoring, possible sanctions and the way in which the revenue from this tax could be spent and redistributed. The collection of the tax comes under the judicial responsibility of each Member State, but the conditions of the international agreement could provide for it to be carried out globally in the same way at the same rate, and as such avoid new tax competition between nation States.

A very low tax can be a prudential monitoring device

Even at a very low rate, the normal tax in the Spahn proposal would function as a monitoring device.

Developing countries could reduce the resources sequestered in official reserves

Most of the small economies lack the capacity to build up sufficient foreign exchange reserves to counter a major attack on their national currency. What they do hold as reserves are generally held in highly liquid and perforce low-return investments in one of the "hard" currencies. This is "immobile capital" until it is needed to protect the currency. If they adopt the circuit breaker tax in the Spahn proposal, those small economies do not need to hold so large an amount of useless capital, because their currency would be protected by the Spahn tax. This gives governments the possibility to invest some of that immobile capital in domestic development.

An ethical argument: taxing capital more and labour less

European and other Western countries generate their revenue mainly through taxes that fall heaviest on labour. Belgium, for example, obtains 60 per cent of its revenue from income tax. If a universal tax were to be applied on capital, the unfair distribution of the taxation burden could gradually be evened out. This would be much more equitable than the current situation.

Lowering the tax burden on labour is also a method for making employment less expensive, without enterprises having to implement new savings. This is a good thing for any economy and helps in fighting unemployment. Lowering the burden of taxation on income would be particularly useful in evening out the gap between men and women; the great majority of women have little or no interest-generating capital.

The CTT is a so-called "blind" tax: the tax itself cannot "see" how large your income or assets are. It is the same for everyone. As it is mainly the wealthy who speculate on changes in the exchange rates of currencies, the tax would not burden ordinary or poor people. From the standpoint of distributive fairness, it is a good instrument for beginning to reduce the gap between the rich and the poor.

3. Next steps

A currency transaction tax, as proposed by Spahn, is thus a desirable instrument to raise revenue that can be dedicated to social and sustainable development purposes. The tax is technically far easier to implement than income tax systems. This proposal concurrently provides a certain amount of revenue, a monitoring device and protection against currency crises. Some governments have successfully put into practice similar measures. Ideally, this domestic tax instrument should function in the context of an international agreement in order to avoid tax competition between different nation States. The advantages of this proposal are gaining respect from an increasing group of experts with international expertise and reputations.

The proposal is also winning more attention in diplomatic circles. Within the United Nations Commission for Social Development and in the monitoring process for the 1995 World Summit for Social Development in Copenhagen, intergovernmental discussions placed this matter on the agenda. It was discussed, in particular, at the Special Session of the United Nations General Assembly held in Geneva from 26 to 30 June 2000 to review progress five years after Copenhagen. The Government of Canada called then for a further study of the Tobin tax to be included as part of the negotiated outcome of the Geneva meeting.

In Geneva, a compromise text was agreed upon, referring to an in-depth study of the advantages and disadvantages of ancillary and new forms of financial sources for development co-operation. When agreement was established over this text, the Canadian and Norwegian governments had it recorded that they actually construed this to mean a study of the Tobin tax. This study is being followed up by the United Nations Secretariat, Caritas Internationalis and CIDSE, along with other non-governmental organizations that will monitor the outcome of this study.

In addition, the CTT was taken up at the regional consultative meeting on financing for development in Asia and the Pacific (Jakarta, 2-5 August 2000). The report on the meeting states: "A proposal was made for a currency transaction tax. Such a tax would simultaneously reduce volatility in the financial market and provide a major source of revenue far in excess of current levels of ODA, for development".[3]

The CTT was discussed at yet another venue. The resolution Joint Parliamentary Assembly on Globalization of the African, Caribbean and Pacific Group of States and the European Union (ACP-EU), adopted on 11 October 2000 in Brussels, Belgium, "considers that the time has come to send out a signal heralding a new departure for the implementation of globalization, and calls therefore on the major industrialized countries and, notably, on the European Union, to introduce a tax on capital transfers as proposed by Professor Tobin" (ACP-EU)(APC-EU 2976/A/00/fin., para. 21).[4]

The International Conference on Financing for Development in 2002 will provide a major opportunity to initiate further concrete steps that have to be monitored by civil society.

References

Cassimon, Danny (1999). Taxing excessive currency speculation to prevent social crisis and finance global challenges. Background paper, Brussels: CIDSE (International Cooperation for Development and Solidarity).

Clunies Ross, Anthony (2000). A tax on foreign-exchange transactions. Report of a consultation held by CIDSE in collaboration with the University of Antwerp (UFSIA), Antwerp, Belgium, 22 October 1999. Brussels: CIDSE. http://www.cidse.org/en/pubs/index.html

Eichengreen, Barry, and Donald Mathieson (1999). *Hedge Funds What Do We Really Know?* Economic Issues No. 19. Washington, D.C.: International Monetary Fund.

International Labour Organization (1998). The social impact of the Asian financial crisis. Technical report for discussion at the High-Level Tripartite Meeting on Social Responses to the Financial Crises in East and South-East Asian Countries, Bangkok, 22-24 April 1998.

Van Liedekerke, Luc (1997). Currency crises, Tobin tax and international justice. Draft paper. University of Antwerp, Centrum voor Ethiek.

Schmidt, Rodney (1999). A feasible foreign exchange transactions tax. Working paper. Ottawa: The North-South Institute.

---

[3] Report of the Regional Consultative Meeting on Financing for Development in the Asia and Pacific Region, Jakarta, 2 to 5 August 2000, para. 65. Available at http://ww.unescap.org/drpad/fin-dev/reportses5.htm.

[4] Available at www.europarl.eu.int/dg2/acp/bru2000/en/resolutions.htm

20

Arbitration to solve the debt problem

KUNIBERT RAFFER[1]

A major initiative is needed in the international community with regard to its management of the debt crises of developing countries. The existing international debt management approach has persisted for too long. The history of sovereign over-indebtedness shows that protracted manœuvring does not turn unpayable debts into paid debt. Large percentages of debt of many countries in crisis must be cancelled, and if a quick and efficient solution is denied, the cost is unnecessary human suffering.

Creditors have already recognized that over-indebted debtors, especially the "heavily indebted poor countries" (HIPCs), will not be able to repay fully, but the unhampered power of creditors prolongs rather than solves the problem. Both the 1996 HIPC Initiative and its 1999 improvement were steps in the right direction, but they also illustrate the problem well. Some features of the Initiative recall—though remotely—customary features of insolvency procedures. However, they fall short of the needs of debtor economies because creditors remain all powerful: judge, jury, bailiff, interested party, witness—occasionally even the debtor's lawyer—all in one. No decent legal system allows this. The very idea of the rule of law prohibits precisely what has happened to sovereign Southern debtors. If the human dignity of people in a debtor country as well as their economic future is to be safeguarded, the decision on how much of the nation's external debt should be written off after a crisis must not be made by the creditors alone, nor by the debtor. Debt crisis resolution must be reached by a fair process balancing the interests of creditors and the sovereign debtor.

---

[1] Professor of Economics, University of Vienna, Austria.

1. Public insolvency under national law

Within all creditor countries insolvency procedures exist. Courts, not creditors, decide on debt reduction. The basic function of any insolvency procedure is to solve a conflict between two fundamental legal principles, using a process chaired by a neutral person or institution. It is the most fundamental principle of the rule of law that one must not be judge in one's own cause. In a situation of over-indebtedness the right of bona fide creditors to interest and repayment collides with the principle recognized by all civilized legal systems that no one must be forced to fulfil contracts (not only regarding loans), if that leads to inhumane distress, endangers one's life or health or violates human dignity. Briefly put, debtors cannot be forced to starve their children to be able to pay more. Although claims are recognized as legitimate, resources are exempted from being seized by bona fide creditors. Human rights and human dignity of debtors, but also an economic fresh start, are given priority over unconditional repayment. It is important to emphasize that insolvency deals with claims based on a solid and proper legal foundation.

The only question is whether such procedures can be used in the case of sovereign debts. Adam Smith advocated it. United States bankruptcy laws provide a useful analytical starting point. Clearly, the insolvency of firms (Chapter 11 of the bankruptcy title of the United States Code) cannot be applied to States. However, Chapter 9 of the bankruptcy title applies to municipalities. Designed and used for decades in the United States as a solution to the problems of debtors vested with governmental powers (i.e., municipalities), the principles of Chapter 9 could be easily applied to sovereign borrowers.

Like all good insolvency laws, the United States law combines the need for a general framework with the flexibility necessary to deal fairly with individual debtors. Introduced in the United States for the very purpose of avoiding the kind of debt management practised internationally, it was refined, for example, after New York City could not file under Chapter 9 in the 1970s because of technicalities, which led to the creation of a *deus ex machina*, the Municipal Assistance Corporation.

2. An international mechanism for sovereign insolvency

Internationally, arbitration, a traditional mechanism of international law, has to serve the role played by national courts in domestic bankruptcy cases. The essential point is that insolvency protection must not be denied to poor people in the South. A fair and transparent arbitration process to resolve debt crises modelled after United States Chapter 9 insolvency is needed, applying the rule of law, the human right of debtor protection and economic efficiency to sovereign debts.[2] As creditors have officially acknowledged both the need for some debtor protection and debt reduction, arbitration remains the one necessary element of a proper and fair solution from which creditors dominating debt management presently still shy away. Proposing international insolvency and proposing arbitration are in my view essentially equivalent as regards solving the problem.

Apart from being an open breach of the rule of law, unrestricted creditor domination is also inefficient from a purely economic perspective. Unsurprisingly, too little has been given too late, and enormous damage has been inflicted on debtor economies. Claims have increased on the books of creditors as a result of continued lending and in some cases from capitalized arrears. As anyone familiar with basic mathematics can verify, creditors who are unwilling to grant sufficient relief when necessary increase the amount of unrecoverable debt. Claims keep growing on paper, further beyond the debtor's economic capacity to repay. "Phantom debts" come into being, existing only on paper, nevertheless damaging the debtor's economic future. They allow creditors to exert pressure, but "forgiving" them does not mean losing money. Money one cannot get cannot be lost. Deleting phantom debts is simply acknowledging economic facts, or "generosity" for free.

Under Chapter 9, United States laws protect both the debtor's governmental powers and the living standards of the indebted municipality's population. Section 904 limits the jurisdiction and powers of domestic courts. The court may not interfere with the choices of a municipality as to what services and benefits it will provide to its inhabitants. The court's jurisdiction depends on the debtor's volition and cannot be extended beyond it. As sovereignty cannot and does not cover more than Section 904, the debtor's situation is de facto like that of a sovereign. Chapter 9 proves that debtor protection can be extended to the population of debtor countries. The openness and transparency of the bargaining process are particularly interesting. Individuals affected by the plan have a right to be heard. Creditors are to receive what can be "reasonably expected" under given circumstances. Their interests have to be taken into account fairly as well. Public interest demands that the debtor must go on functioning as a public entity providing basic services in fields such as health, welfare or security to its population.

---

[2]   More detailed information in English, French, Spanish and German is available from the author at http://mailbox.univie.ac.at/~rafferk5.

The arbitration mechanism

To start the process before a neutral arbitration panel, sovereign debtors might "file" for debt arbitration/insolvency proceedings by depositing this demand at the United Nations, for example, with the Secretary-General. Clearly, only debtor governments would have the right to file, and it would be their sovereign decision to do so. Beyond serving as the organization where a sovereign debtor can file its request for an arbitration process, the United Nations could play an important role in organizing the nomination of arbitrators by the two parties, possibly also providing limited secretariat services needed by them. The creditors and the debtor would be invited to nominate an equal number of arbitrators, who in turn would elect one more member to reach an uneven number (ideally not more than five).

Once established, the arbitration panel would proceed according to the main principles of United States Chapter 9, deciding on procedural matters as they came up. Since these principles could be applied immediately, no further technical work would be required. An independent entity, the arbitration panel, not creditors, would have the power to decide finally on the sovereign debt workout, if no agreement should be reached voluntarily. The affected population would have a voice for exercising its right to be heard, being represented by such entities as non-governmental organizations (NGOs), trade unions, employers' associations, grassroots organizations, or international organizations, such as UNICEF.

Presently, both creditors and debtors employ qualified personnel managing reschedulings or other debt-related issues. In an international Chapter 9 these people would simply do what they have done so far, except that they would negotiate and argue their points before a temporary arbitration panel instead of among themselves.

Once a workable debt work-out plan is agreed upon, the panel can be dissolved. No permanent bureaucracy would come into being. If further disagreements should develop later on, the same persons (or, if necessary, other arbitrators) could reconvene to solve the issue(s).

Precedents for arbitration of debt workouts

Arbitration by a neutral body is the basic element of a fair and humane solution to a dispute, according to the principles presently used in various international arrangements. Arbitration is increasingly applied to solve international problems by the World Trade Organization or North American Free Trade Agreement. Governments of the Organisation for Economic Co-operation and Development wanted to make arbitration part and parcel of the Multilateral Agreement on Investment.

Arbitration has also already been part of international debt arrangements, such as the London Accord of 1953 with Germany.[3] Loan agreements in the 1930s routinely stipulated arbitration to solve disagreements. Agreements between Nigeria and Uruguay with private creditors are examples in the recent past.

In addition, a publication by Commerzbank in Germany stated that private creditors would not object to debt reduction by arbitration in cases of extreme debtor distress, if it is fair and the burden is shared appropriately among all creditors. It pointed out that this was presently not the case, as official international financial institutions (International Monetary Fund, World Bank, regional development banks) managing debt renegotiations have privileged their own claims over those of all other creditors.[4] Being creditors themselves, these institutions cannot fulfil the role of arbitrators.

Protecting the poor and recovery

Schemes to protect a minimum standard of living must be part of every international debt workout plan. In analogy to the protection granted to the population of an indebted municipality by United States Chapter 9, the money to service a country's debts must not be raised by destroying basic social services. Subsidies and transfers necessary to guarantee humane minimum standards for the poor must be maintained. Funds necessary for sustainable economic recovery must be set aside. The principle of debtor protection demands the exemption of resources necessary to finance minimum standards for basic health services, primary education and other basic needs. This exemption can only be justified if that money is demonstrably used for its declared purpose. Not without reason, NGOs as well as creditors are concerned that this might not be the case.

A transparently managed fund, as proposed by Ann Pettifor of Jubilee 2000 UK, financed by the debtor in domestic currency would guarantee that money freed from debt servicing is used for the poor and for expenditures necessary for the economic recovery of the sovereign debtor. Its management could be monitored by an international board consisting of members from the debtor and creditor countries. Its members could be nominated by NGOs and governments, including the debtor's. As this fund would be a legal entity of its own, it would operate independently from the government. Similarly, neither

---

[3] By the way, my argument in 1987 that internationally neutral arbitration panels must serve the function of bankruptcy courts was based on Germany's example.

[4] There is no dispute that these official institutions enjoy preferred creditor status — Eds.

management nor the board of the fund would be concerned with decisions on the government's budget, which is an important part of a country's sovereignty.

3. Conclusion

The kind of arbitration proposed here would fulfil the demands of donor governments: participation, transparency and respect for the rule of law. Its adoption would also be a necessary part of a meaningful change in the international financial architecture. Its very existence would strongly discourage excessive lending by creditors who otherwise assume that sovereign loans will always be repaid eventually.

Arbitration could enter into debt policy with the stroke of a pen if powerful creditor governments agreed. Thus, advocacy by the United Nations and NGOs is necessary. Both human rights and the rule of law demand a fair and open arbitration process modelled after United States Chapter 9 to recreate the preconditions for development and for reducing poverty. No difficult and costly legal or administrative framework is necessary. The Paris Club functions without a legal base. Only the will of important creditor countries is needed. Sadly, arbitration—quite popular in other cases—is denied when it comes to applying the human right of debtor protection and the rule of law to the poorest in developing countries. Without such an orderly and fair process, crises are prolonged and damage is inflicted unnecessarily, mostly to the poorest, so-called vulnerable groups. People in debtor countries need justice and economic sense, not generosity— the same protection of their basic needs and human dignity any other debtor enjoys. Put in a nutshell, whoever on this globe looks like a human being should be treated as one.

21

Strengthening the Economic and Social Council

JULIAN DISNEY[1]

Serious weaknesses in the international structures and processes for cooperation on economic policy are major reasons for the persistent lack of adequate financing for development in poorer countries and the alarming increases in inequality between rich and poor countries. These weaknesses cause severe personal hardship for very many people, especially in developing countries, often with fatal consequences. They also harm many business enterprises that want to compete on fair terms and many governments that want to advance the interests of their citizens.

The United Nations has a clear mandate and responsibility to play a major role in international economic cooperation, especially through the Economic and Social Council (ECOSOC). Yet from its earliest years, ECOSOC has largely failed to do so. Instead, the major roles have been played by organizations such as the International Monetary Fund (IMF), World Bank, Group of Seven (G7) and the Organization for Economic Cooperation and Development (OECD), which are dominated by the wealthiest countries and commonly give insufficient attention in their decision-making to the importance of social development and environmental sustainability. The World Trade Organization (WTO) has behaved in a similar way, although its 1999 Seattle meeting demonstrated that developing countries can have some impact in international organizations if they have a majority of the votes, organize themselves effectively and enjoy strong civil society support.

---

[1]   International Council on Social Welfare, Australia.

1.   From Copenhagen to Seattle to New York

The World Summit for Social Development, held in Copenhagen in 1995, agreed that there should be greater international cooperation in the development and implementation of economic and social policies. The Summit reaffirmed the central coordinating role that the United Nations system, especially the Economic and Social Council, should play in pursuing these goals. That role was specified more than fifty years ago in the Charter of the United Nations. The Summit emphasized that the structures, resources and processes of ECOSOC should be strengthened substantially, and that the World Bank, IMF, WTO and the International Labour Organization (ILO) should cooperate with it more closely.

Some progress has been made in the directions that were agreed in Copenhagen, especially since the financial crises of 1997 and 1998. For example, the World Bank and IMF have engaged a little more closely with ECOSOC (including annual meetings), and the two Bretton Woods institutions have made more frequent references to the importance of social issues, especially poverty reduction. Sometimes, at least with the Bank, the new words have been accompanied by improved practices. The Financial Stability Forum and the Group of 20 (G20) have been established to strengthen international coordination on some aspects of financial regulation. As with WTO, however, they are outside the UN system and lack adequate mechanisms for giving due weight to the interests of less powerful countries and of social development or environmental considerations.

ECOSOC has sought since Copenhagen to strengthen its involvement in international consideration of macroeconomic issues. There have been some improvements in its internal processes and those of its relevant commissions, such as the Commission on Sustainable Development and the Commission for Social Development. In general, however, the Council continues to have very little influence on major issues of economic policy. Its impact on social policy is somewhat greater, especially as it coordinates a wide range of international agencies, but it continues to focus excessively on process rather than substance. Even among those people around the world who work on issues within ECOSOC's ambit, a very small proportion are aware of its existence.

The confrontations in Seattle in 1999 were seen widely as a powerful challenge to the World Trade Organization. But they also presented a challenge—and opportunity—for the United Nations. A central debate was whether WTO, ILO or some combination of the two should be responsible for resolving possible conflicts between trade rules and labour standards.

Concerns were also expressed about how environmental considerations would be taken into account. Of course, many other issues such as health, education and poverty reduction can also be crucially affected by trade rules.

Similar concerns about a lack of diversity and balance in the composition of groups such as G7 and IMF, and their tendency to give primacy to narrow economic interests at the expense of other considerations, have led to intense and widespread public protests in recent years in many different places around the world. Here again, there is both a challenge and an opportunity for the United Nations.

The mechanisms for resolving conflicts between different bodies of rules and different sectors of interests, such as those that arose in Seattle, should not be determined by mechanisms that are designed as ad hoc responses to particular political forces at particular moments in time. Instead, they should be resolved through an ongoing and coherent framework for discussion and decision-making that is established and overseen by an entity that recognizes the full range of relevant issues and interests.

At the national level, this overarching role is commonly played by the head of government, cabinet, or some other "whole-of-government" authority. They may examine and decide upon the substantive issue, or they may prescribe and supervise mechanisms and criteria by which it is to be decided. At the global level, ECOSOC's mandate, composition and location within the United Nations system make it the most appropriate body to have this type of overarching responsibility for determining particular conflicts in international rules and standards on economic and social issues or for supervising their determination by other means.

2. A wider ECOSOC role in economic issues and a strengthened ECOSOC

ECOSOC needs to become more closely and centrally involved in key issues such as financial market regulation, tax policy and administration, corporate regulation and other aspects of economic policy of global importance. This was recognized to some extent at the Copenhagen Summit and has become even more crucial as economic globalization and the interdependence of nations has continued to develop.

Policies and practices in these areas have suffered severely from the dominance of narrow economic perspectives, and of the wealthiest countries, in key organizations such as the World Bank, IMF and WTO. Their failures have not only retarded social development but have also, as can be seen in the widespread financial crises of recent years, hindered longer-term economic development.

In principle, ECOSOC should be less prone to the weaknesses of these other organizations. Most of its members are from developing countries, and its mandate covers a very wide range of both economic and social issues. It should, therefore, be able to arrive at relatively broad-based and balanced assessments, especially with the assistance of the wide range of agencies within its system. In practice, however, these potential strengths have been major causes of ECOSOC's ineffectiveness. Its breadth of representation has been achieved by becoming so large as to militate against the kinds of detailed, frank and informal negotiations that are often essential for resolution of the most important and contentious issues. The breadth of its responsibilities, coupled with its size and inadequate procedures, has also contributed to a general lack of focus, expertise and momentum on major policy issues, especially in the economic sphere.

Moreover, because the wealthiest countries do not have the control that they enjoy in bodies such as the World Bank and IMF, they have not wished ECOSOC to play a major role on substantial economic issues.

These and other weaknesses have evoked a number of calls in recent years for ECOSOC to be strengthened or replaced by a new Council. For example, the independent Commission on Global Governance recommended in 1995 that ECOSOC should be replaced by an Economic Security Council which would be smaller in size and would provide standing membership for the most economically powerful countries while also improving methods for regional selection of the other members. Other observers have made broadly similar proposals but with differing titles for the new body.

Less radical and specific calls for strengthening ECOSOC rather than replacing it, were made last year at the Twenty-fourth Special Session of the General Assembly on implementation of the Copenhagen Summit, as well as in the Millennium Declaration. Some significant suggestions for improving ECOSOC processes were made by the Secretary-General of the United Nations in his report of 18 December 2000 to the Preparatory Committee for the High-level International Intergovernmental Event on Financing for Development.

The remainder of this paper outlines four key areas that could be considered as possibilities for reform. They include improving the basic processes of the Council and its Bureau; developing expert high-level working groups; restructuring the Council itself or replacing it with a new Council; and strengthening interaction with regional groupings.

Improving processes

Despite some recent improvements, many of the basic ECOSOC processes continue to be unsuited for a body with its crucial, wide-ranging and sometimes urgent responsibilities. While the Council itself might be considered too large, its five-member Bureau is too small. Moreover, the Bureau commonly does not have any representative from one of the more economically powerful or populous countries. The Bureau could be expanded to eight or ten members, thus increasing its ability to achieve sufficient representativeness and authority, handle its workload and play a more vigorous leadership role.

ECOSOC's main substantive meeting occurs only once each year but then lasts for four weeks. If the Council is to play an effective role on key issues in the modern world, it should abbreviate its current annual meeting and hold other meetings at more frequent intervals, perhaps quarterly. It could also focus more on detailed discussion of key policy issues rather than continuing to devote so much of its time to somewhat ritualized consideration of operational reports from its constituent organizations. Appropriate non-government experts and representatives should be invited to be full participants in some of these discussions although without, of course, any right to vote.

ECOSOC should also make greater efforts to achieve active involvement in its work by senior ministers. This would be aided if, especially when meeting at the ministerial level, it did so principally through round-table discussion and decision-making on a few key issues rather than, as happens at the current "high-level sessions", through a series of set-piece speeches on widely varying topics from the floor of a large hall. The current processes for ECOSOC meetings do little to attract repeat visits by ministers who are more interested in productivity than protocol and who are already heavily committed and influential in their own countries.

Developing special working groups

The quality and impact of ECOSOC's work would be substantially enhanced if it made greater use of special working groups on key issues. This applies especially in economic areas in which there is no existing ECOSOC commission that would be appropriate for such a role.

For example, a special working group on economic cooperation could be established, with broad responsibilities including oversight of ECOSOC interaction with organizations such as the World Bank, IMF, WTO and G20. Another option is to establish a special working group on international cooperation on tax reform, which would respond to the growing realization of the need for a globally balanced international forum in this area.

Special working groups of this kind could have about 25 members, comprising approximately equal representation of the most economically powerful countries (the G7), the most populous countries (such as Brazil, China, India and the Russian Federation) and representatives of the other countries chosen on a regional basis. This is similar to the composition proposed by the Commission on Global Governance for its Economic Security Council. It also bears considerable similarity to the new Group of 20 but with the crucial addition of regionally elected representatives from all parts of the world rather than the European Union alone.

Special working groups could be established initially for a fixed term or on a permanent basis. In order to be effective on key issues, they would need to meet at least every few months, preferably in different venues around the world, and involve ministers or other high-level representatives with political authority. This contrasts, for example, with the existing ECOSOC committee on international cooperation on tax matters, which consists of technical tax experts and meets at lengthy intervals.

Restructuring or replacing the Council

There may be much to be said for reducing the size of ECOSOC and changing its composition, so that it resembles the type of Economic Security Council proposed by the Commission on Global Governance and others. This would reflect the need for a Council that is small enough to be effective, yet provides a reasonably fair and realistic balance of representation.

Such a change, however, would require modification of Article 61 of the Charter of the United Nations, which has already been amended twice to increase the size of ECOSOC. Although it would tend to strengthen rather than weaken the proportion and effectiveness of developing country representation, the proposal is unlikely to attract sufficient support from this quarter in the near future. At least some of the major economic powers are also likely to oppose it, if only because they do not want the United Nations to become substantially more influential on economic issues. These sources of opposition would be even stronger in relation to replacing ECOSOC with a new Council.

Much progress may be achievable, however, by securing agreement to establish one or more special working groups of the kind mentioned earlier. The new groups would remain subject to ultimate oversight by the full Council in its current form and there would be no need to amend the Charter. But their smaller size and narrower remit would make them more likely than the full Council of more than fifty members to develop sufficient focus, expertise and authority in their key area of responsibility.

Strengthening interaction with regional groups

Whether or not its composition is changed, ECOSOC should substantially strengthen its interaction with key regional groupings such as the European Union (EU), Mercosur, the Association of South East Asian Nations (ASEAN), the Southern African Development Community (SADC) and others. These groupings are commonly more significant to heads of government and other senior ministers, and more reflective of appropriate regional boundaries, than most of ECOSOC's longer-standing regional commissions.

ECOSOC's profile and impact as a global body could be strengthened substantially by convening an annual regional consultation involving not only its own regional commissions but also the other, non-UN groupings. Some of these groupings might also serve as a basis for selection of regional representatives on ECOSOC and its special working groups; some are already acting increasingly as negotiating groups within ECOSOC processes and, for example, played influential roles at the World Trade Organization meeting in Seattle. Developments of these kinds can be seen as consistent with a concept of international governance that might be called "constructive regionalism".

Constructive regionalism

The concept of constructive regionalism is "constructive" in the sense of encouraging regions to be positive in their engagement with other parts of the world rather than merely defensive and exclusive. It is also "constructive" in the sense of developing regional structures that could be building blocks for a global framework of cooperation that strikes an appropriate balance between globalization and local autonomy.

Among other things, constructive regionalism can help to maximize the benefits of internationalization in economic and other fields while also helping to minimize the dangers. It also can be an important way of strengthening South-South cooperation, as recognized by developing countries in the 1998 Bali Declaration on Regional and Subregional Economic Cooperation of the Developing Countries and reiterated at the historic Group of 77 South Summit in Havana in 2000.

The European Union has already established substantial power and influence within its own region and the world. Its development constitutes recognition by some of the most powerful countries in the world that they must join in such a grouping if they are adequately to develop their capabilities and protect their interests. The need for such realism and regional cooperation is surely even greater for developing countries.

The EU and some other regional groupings are already very active in developing bi-regional interaction. As regional groupings develop further in significance, so will bi-regional and multi-regional processes. It is essential, however, for these developments to occur in an appropriate global framework, rather than in ways that heighten tension and inequity. Hence the emphasis above on encouraging new regional groupings to interact more closely with, and operate as negotiating groups within, the ECOSOC system in ways similar to the current practice of EU countries.

3. The way ahead

Recent systemic failures by bodies such as IMF and WTO have given the United Nations its best opportunity for several decades, perhaps ever, to play the kind of major role in international economic policy-making that it was intended to play. Its fulfilment of that role is essential in the interests of sustainable and equitable development around the world. It is greatly in the interests of developing countries, in particular, to agree speedily on a package of specific and hard-headed proposals for strengthening ECOSOC and to vigorously pursue their implementation.

4. Summary of proposals for strengthening the ECOSOC system

- The ECOSOC Bureau should be enlarged and encouraged to play a more vigorous leadership role.
- ECOSOC should increase the frequency of its meetings, abbreviate its annual meeting, focus more on in-depth policy discussion than on formal consideration of operational agency reports and give greater opportunities for effective participation in some of its discussions by non-governmental experts and representatives.
- ECOSOC should establish special working groups, involving ministers or other representatives with high political authority, and make greater use of independent expert advisory panels to develop the Council's expertise and influence, especially in areas of major economic policy.
- In particular, ECOSOC should establish a special working group on economic cooperation of about 25 members, of whom one third are standing members comprising G7 countries, another one third are standing members comprising countries with very large populations and the other one third are elected triennially by the remaining countries on a regional basis.
- ECOSOC should also consider establishing a special working group on international cooperation on tax reform and seek more active involve-

ment in consideration of issues relating to business regulation.

- ECOSOC should convene an annual regional consultation involving non-UN regional groupings such as EU, SADC, Mercosur and ASEAN as well as the ECOSOC regional commissions.
- These regional groupings should also be encouraged and assisted to operate as elective and negotiating groups within ECOSOC processes.
- After experience of these reforms, consideration could be given to amending the Charter of the United Nations in order to reduce ECOSOC to about half of its current size of 54 members, with its new composition being similar to the proposal above in relation to the special working group on economic cooperation.

References

Commission on Global Governance (1995). *Our Global Neighbourhood,* chaps. 4 and 5. Oxford, England and New York: Oxford University Press.

Disney, J. (2000). Sustainable Social Progress. Paper presented at the International Symposium, Partnership for Social Development in a Globalizing World, Geneva, 27 June 2000. Montreal, Canada: International Council on Social Welfare.

_____ (2000a). Agencies of change: Should ECOSOC be Reformed ? *United Nations Chronicle,* vol. XXXVII, No. 2.

_____ (2000b). A reformed ECOSOC for a stronger UN. *The Social Development Review,* vol. 4, No. 3 (September 2000), pp.1-2.

Global Governance Reform Project (2000). *Reimagining the Future: Towards Democratic Governance.* Bundoora, Victoria, Australia: La Trobe University.

Grey, W. (2000). *UN Jigsaw,* New York: Vantage Press.

Jeong, Ho-Won (1998). The struggle in the UN System for wider participation in forming global economic polices. In *The Future of the United Nations System: Potential for the Twenty-first Century,* C. Alger, ed. Tokyo: United Nations University Press.

United Nations (1995). Copenhagen Declaration on Social Development, commitment No. 10, and Programme of Action of the World Summit for Social Development, para.95f. *Report of the World Summit for Social Development, Copenhagen, 6-12 March 1995.* Sales No. E.96.IV.8.

United Nations, General Assembly (2000). Further initiatives for social development. Resolution S24/2 (1 July 2000), para. 149.

_____ (2000a). Millennium declaration. Resolution 55/2, (8 September 2000), para. 30.

United Nations, General Assembly, Preparatory Committee on Financing for Development (2001). Report of the Secretary-General to the Preparatory Committee for the High-level International Intergovernmental Event on Financing for Development (A/AC.257/12), paras. 168-177.

Notes on the contributors

Tariq Banuri is Senior Research Director, Stockholm Environment Institute - Boston. His work focuses on sustainable development policy. He is a leading member of two of the largest professional networks in this area: the Inter-governmental Panel on Climate Change (IPCC), on which he is a convening Lead Author, and the World Conservation Union (IUCN), where he is the elected chair of the Commission on Environmental, Economic, and Social Policy (CEESP). At the FfD Hearings he represented the Regional and International Networking Group of organizations working for sustainable development (The RING).

Bart Bode is Head of the Policy Department of Broederlijk Delen, a development and advocacy organization associated with the Flemish Church and member of International Cooperation for Development and Solidarity *(Coopération Internationale pour le Développement et la Solidarité* [CIDSE]), an international coalition of 14 Catholic organizations working together with other groups and partners in the South and the North on development issues.

Marshall Carter is the Chairman of the Board of the State Street Bank and Trust Company and its holding company, the State Street Corporation. State Street's core business is financial custody, which it provides to customers in over 90 markets around the world. Mr. Carter joined State Street in July 1991 as President and Chief Operating Officer. He became Chief Executive Officer in 1992 and Chairman in 1993. During his nine-year tenure as CEO, the company has grown tenfold.

Julian Disney is former President of the International Council on Social Welfare (ICSW). Founded in 1928 in Paris, ICSW is a global non-governmental organization that represents a wide range of national and international member organizations that seek to advance social welfare, social development and social justice.

April Fehling was until recently a Research Associate at the Development Group for Alternative Policies (The Development GAP), based in the United States. The Development GAP aims to ensure that the knowledge, priorities and efforts of the women and men of the South inform the decisions made in the North about their economies and the environments in which they live. In her previous work while a Fulbright Scholar in India, Fehling researched gender and development issues.

Karen Hansen-Kuhn is Trade Program Coordinator of the Development Group for Alternative Policies (The Development GAP) and, in that capacity, serves as International Coordinator for the United States coalition, the Alliance for Responsible Trade.

Rodney Harper is Customer Awareness Director for the Alcatel Group's operations covering France, Africa, the Middle East, Turkey, Central Asia and the Indian subcontinent. From 1998 to 2000, he was Project Director for the same geographical regions and, in the past, held a number of senior techno-commercial, international marketing management positions addressing the concerns of the developing world. Alcatel, a major telecommunications and Internet firm based in France, has a strong local presence in 130 countries.

Douglas Hellinger is the Executive Director of the Development Group for Alternative Policies (The Development GAP) based in the United States. He is also Global Coordinator of the Structural Adjustment Participatory Review International Network (SAPRIN), which is the civil society network that is working with governments and the World Bank on a joint review of structural adjustment programmes. The Development GAP aims to ensure that the knowledge, priorities and efforts of the women and men of the South inform the decisions made in the North about their economies and the environments in which they live.

Barry Herman is Chief of the Finance and Development Branch, Development Policy Analysis Division, in the Department of Economic and Social Affairs of the United Nations Secretariat. He participates actively in the substantive work undertaken by the Financing for Development Coordinating Secretariat.

Cheryl Hesse is Vice President and Senior Counsel of Capital International, Inc., a leading United States investor in emerging market securities. She joined the legal department of Capital International's parent, the Capital Group Companies, in 1994. Ms. Hesse focuses on corporate and securities matters and chairs Capital International's Corporate Governance Working Group.

Hanns Michael Hoelz is the Global Head of Public Relations and the Global Head of Sustainable Development for Deutsche Bank Group, a major international financial service provider, with more than 12 million customers in over 70 countries. Mr. Hoelz represents Deutsche Bank in a number of national and international committees, including the steering committee of the United Nations Environment Programme.

Jenny Kimmis has worked as a researcher in the Policy Department of Oxfam GB. Founded in 1942 as the Oxford Committee for Famine Relief, Oxfam GB is the original member of an international network of non-governmental development organizations. Ms. Kimmis is currently working for the Institute of Development Studies at the University of Sussex in the United Kingdom.

Ruth Mayne has been a policy advisor for Oxfam GB since 1993. Her work involves research and advocacy on international trade, investment and employment issues.

Tom Marshella is a Managing Director for Moody's Investors Service. His responsibilities include project and infrastructure finance, bank loan ratings and high yield analysis. Between 1993 and 1996, he headed the infrastructure and project finance initiatives of Moody's throughout Asia and the Pacific. Moody's is one of the leading providers of credit ratings, research and financial information to global capital markets.

Jens Martens is the representative to the United Nations of the World Economy, Ecology and Development Association (WEED). Based in Germany, WEED was created as a service and consulting body to improve the performance of non-governmental organizations working on North-South development issues. It cooperates with NGOs, grassroots and popular organizations on both the national and the international levels.

Thomas Niles is the President of the United States Council for International Business, which is the US affiliate of the International Chamber of Commerce. He assumed this position in February 1999. He was previously in the United States Foreign Service; he has also served as Ambassador to Canada, the European Union and Greece, and was Assistant Secretary of State for Europe and Canada.

Federica Pietracci works as civil society focal point in the Financing for Development Coordinating Secretariat in the Department of Economic and Social Affairs of the United Nations Secretariat. She previously worked for the Secretariat of the United Nations Commission on Sustainable Development, where the focus of her work was the involvement of "major groups" of society in the implementation of Agenda 21.

Marina Ponti is Policy Adviser for External Relations of Mani Tese, an Italian non-governmental development organization operating at the national and international level to further justice, solidarity and respect among peoples.

Kunibert Raffer is Associate Professor at the Department of Economics of the University of Vienna. His areas of research include international trade, international finance, debt and aid.

Zo Randriamaro is the Programme Manager of the Gender and Economic Reforms in Africa (GERA) Programme at Third World Network-Africa. Third World Network-Africa is an independent non-profit international network of organizations and individuals concerned with development, the third world and North-South issues.

Roberto Rubio-Fabián is the Executive Director of the National Development Foundation of El Salvador (*FUNDE*). He coordinates the Structural Adjustment Participatory Review International Network (SAPRIN) in Latin America, which is the civil society network that is working with governments and the World Bank on a joint review of structural adjustment programmes.

Krishnan Sharma is an international economist in the Financing for Development Coordinating Secretariat in the Department of Economic and Social Affairs of the United Nations Secretariat. He is the focal point for the dialogue between governments and business-sector stakeholders on financing for development issues.

Chulakorn Singhakowin is President and Chief Executive Officer of the Bank of Asia PCL, a major Thai commercial bank, and Chairman of the Thai Bankers Association. Mr. Singhakowin started his banking career in 1974 with Bangkok Bank and has worked in several countries. He joined the Bank of Asia in 1995 and was appointed its President and CEO in 1992.

Erika Spanger-Siegfried is a research associate with Stockholm Environment Institute (SEI-Boston), and focuses on the intersection of sustainable development and international environmental policy, with special emphasis on the impact of climate change. At the FfD Hearings, she collaborated with the Regional and International Networking Group of organizations working for sustainable development (The RING).

Victor Valdepeñas is the President and Chief Operating Officer of the Union Bank of the Philippines, a major commercial bank headquartered in Manila. He is also a past President of the Foreign Exchange Association of the Philippines and of the Philippine Economic Society.

Andre van Heemstra is a Director at Unilever and a member of the firm's Executive Committee. He has had a long and distinguished career with the company and until recently was President of its East Asia Pacific Group. He has also worked at a senior level in Kenya and Turkey. Unilever is a diversified consumer products company, selling home, personal care and food products in 150 countries to over 150 million customers per day.

Mariama Williams is a visiting researcher at the Centre of Concern in Washington, D.C. At the hearings she also represented the International Network for Gender and Trade: Development Alternatives with Women for a New Era (DAWN); and DAWN—Caribbean.

John de Wit is the founder and Managing Director of the Small Enterprise Foundation, a non-governmental microfinance institution based in the Northern Province of South Africa. In the field of microcredit, the Small Enterprise Foundation has gained a worldwide reputation for its dedication to reaching the very poor, those who live below half the national poverty line. It seeks to ensure a positive impact through the provision of group-based microcredit and the promotion of regular savings.

Davide Zanoni is assistant researcher in macroeconomics at the Cattaneo University of Castellanza, Varese, Italy, and collaborates with Mani Tese, an Italian non-governmental development organization operating at the national and international level to further justice, solidarity and respect among peoples.

Index

Catalogue Request

Name: _____

Address: _____

Tel: _____

Fax: _____

E-mail: _____

To receive a catalogue of UNU Press publications kindly photocopy this form and send or fax it back to us with your details. You can also e-mail us this information. Please put "Mailing List" in the subject line.

 **United Nations University Press**

53-70, Jingumae 5-chome
Shibuya-ku, Tokyo 150-8925, Japan
Tel: +81-3-3499-2811 Fax: +81-3-3406-7345
E-mail: sales@hq.unu.edu http://www.unu.edu